WASIM

THE AUTOBIOGRAPHY OF
WASIM AKRAM

WASIM

THE AUTOBIOGRAPHY OF
WASIM AKRAM

PIATKUS

To my father,
Ch-Mohammad Akram

First published in hardback in 1998 by
Judy Piatkus (Publishers) Ltd
5 Windmill Street, London W1P 1HF

The moral right of the author has been asserted

A catalogue record for this book is available from the British Library

ISBN 0-7499-1808-X

Designed by Paul Saunders
Typeset by Phoenix Photosetting, Chatham, Kent
Printed and bound in Great Britain by
Mackays of Chatham PLC, Chatham, Kent

Contents

Acknowledgements

So many people have helped me throughout my life and cricket career. Above all, I would like to thank my parents and grandparents in Lahore for their love and support, and, in the case of my grandmother, for allowing me to neglect my studies in favour of playing cricket in the street! My wife, Huma, has given me stability and sound advice throughout the ten years I have known her.

I'm so grateful to various cricketers from an older generation who saw something in me, particularly Khalid Mahmood, Khan Mohammad, Agha Saadat and Saud Khan. Without Javed Miandad sticking out his neck on my behalf when I was just eighteen, I might never have had the chance to break into the Pakistan side. And without Imran Khan's constant support and guidance, I would have learned very little.

My time in England, playing for Lancashire, has been great fun. All the officials and players at this great club have been so kind to me. From day one, they have made me welcome and treated me as if I was part of one big family. My cricket education has also been extended by playing for so long at Old Trafford, and I hope that England supporters don't feel too strongly about that!

My thanks also to my business adviser in Manchester, Peter Johnson. And to my friend, Guhlan Mehdi, who looked after Huma and I so devotedly in the summer of 1997 at home in Manchester, when I was feeling sorry for myself with a serious shoulder injury and my poor wife was heavily pregnant, counting the days!

Finally, my thanks go to the BBC's Patrick Murphy for finding the time, in between Test matches, to negotiate the M6 motorway and get my thoughts down on tape. Putting them in a coherent order and making me sound sensible was an even greater effort.

Wasim Akram
March 1998

CHAPTER 1

Out in the Cold

AT THE start of 1998, I was a fulfilled cricketer. At the age of thirty-one, I was captain of Pakistan and looking forward to my new responsibilities as captain of Lancashire in a few months' time. I was at my peak as a player, having recovered from a worrying shoulder injury to take wickets and lead my country to a thumping three-nil Test series win over the West Indies just a few weeks earlier. Yet, within the space of a few days, my world had been turned upside down. My reputation had been so blackened by baseless allegations that I couldn't take the pressure any more. So I resigned the captaincy of my country. That was a big enough blow, but when I was dropped as a player, I was shattered. The selectors decided I would not go on our tour to South Africa and Zimbabwe and I was given no explanation. It was a particularly difficult time as I had no idea why I hadn't been selected. After fourteen years as an international player, I was dumped, and to make matters worse, nobody was acting on my behalf to scotch the innuendos about my integrity as a cricketer. It was the lowest period of my career, at a time when surely I ought to have been on top of the world, with so much ahead to motivate me.

The fact that I was reinstated to the Pakistan team at the start of March for the last Test in South Africa didn't make me entirely happy, or lead me to believe I had been vindicated. I was brought back because I alone pressed my case at the highest level in Pakistan. The allegations against me couldn't be sustained, so I was

1

given the benefit of the doubt. That's not the same as being declared innocent and that is still my aim.

I found out that I hadn't been picked for the South Africa tour through Teletext in London. That's right – no one in a position of authority in Pakistan cricket had contacted me with the bad news before I flew to England to launch my benefit year with Lancashire. When I arrived in London, I switched on the television and saw that I had been cast aside. Intrigues and gossip are never far away in Pakistan cricket and I became another casualty. The situation got so worrying that I received death and kidnap threats, along with other members of my family. Back home in Lahore, I needed two guards outside my house. On more than one occasion, my father, two brothers and I would pick up the phone and hear someone say, 'We're going to pick you up and shoot you.' My four nieces were threatened at school, while my father was told he was going to be kidnapped and a huge ransom would be demanded. My family live in two houses in Lahore a couple of minutes away from each other, and all we could do during those awful days was huddle together for comfort and support, hoping we would get some peace and respect for our privacy eventually. We simply had to ride it out, and one way to do that was to resign the captaincy of my country – with huge regret. It was a crazy time, and I wouldn't wish it on anybody.

And why did all this happen? Simple: the obsession with gambling that dominates cricket in Pakistan and India. It's now such a feverish, obsessive activity that if you lose a cricket match, you are blamed for also losing fortunes for people, and ruining their lives. I know of gamblers in Pakistan who have lost their businesses as a result of this epidemic, yet they can't kick the habit. Many who place bets on cricket just don't understand the subtleties of the game. Cricket is on the television almost every day in Pakistan – not just internationals, but veterans' and womens' tournaments – so there is always scope to make a fortune. And to lose one. The press fan the flames with rumours and ill-researched statements that a certain player is sure to do well in the upcoming match, and many uneducated, naive readers lay down money on such information. One-day cricket is now so popular in Pakistan that vast crowds watch it on television, or pack the grounds. Many of those watchers don't realise that fortunes fluctuate so wildly and so quickly in one-day games because of their very nature: pressure can get to players and they do rash things that seem corrupt to gamblers who are simply obsessed with winning a bet, rather than enjoying the twists and turns of a cricket match.

So I got sucked into this frenetic gambling atmosphere because I committed the cardinal sin of losing a couple of one-day matches as Pakistan captain. It all blew up in December 1997 when four international teams played in the Sharjah Trophy. Under my leadership, Pakistan were well fancied, and vast sums of money were placed on us, as individuals and as a successful team. Yet we played poorly, losing to England and the West Indies, although we were pleased to beat our arch rivals, India. I didn't captain the side as well as I would have liked. Our batting order wasn't right in the England game, and in retrospect I should have sent in Azhar Mahmood ahead of me at number eight. I scratched around for nineteen balls to make only four, and we lost by eight runs when we really ought to have won. Against West Indies, I dropped two simple catches, bowled poorly, and was involved in two run-outs that were my fault. Fair enough – I had a bad series in a tournament in which I usually do very well. That's cricket, it happens. So we lost, despite trying our best. End of story? Not a bit of it.

When we got back to Pakistan, the temperature had really risen. Former Test players had put their names to newspaper articles, saying that the reason we had lost in Sharjah was because we had taken bribes to throw the games. I was right in the firing line, as captain and all-rounder who had performed below par in the tournament. Some papers reported as a matter of fact that I had made a lot of money out of losing those two games, and that one of my brothers is a bookmaker, so he had the inside track. It didn't seem to matter that neither of my brothers has ever been a bookmaker. The fact that some former players had castigated me in the press gave these amazing allegations credibility. It was all sadly reminiscent of 1996, when Pakistan lost in the World Cup quarter-final against India in Bangalore. I had to withdraw through a painful rib injury and when we lost, the rumours started that I had taken a bribe to stand down, and defeat for us also made me a small fortune. That had really hurt, and the subsequent events when my house was stoned and my family threatened only added to my

3

misery. I really don't know how these people can imagine that I could influence the result of a match in which I wasn't even playing.

I have never attempted to throw a match, and have never even considered such a thing for a second. I also have no knowledge of any Pakistan player taking money to influence events on the field. That is a slur that just won't go away in Pakistan cricket, and it claimed Salim Malik when he was sacked as captain. Salim has always protested his innocence and I have no reason to doubt him. That didn't save his neck, though, and the relentless drip of rumours also forced me to resign as Pakistan captain. I just couldn't take the strain of dealing with such smears on my reputation. I have always prided myself on my strong competitive streak and integrity of my performance and the very notion that I would take a bribe filled me with horror. The fact that some sections of the press stirred up the rumours depressed and angered me intensely. Could they not consider for a moment the obvious pride I had shown in representing my country? Didn't they understand that in my long career I had earned a comfortable amount of money and would not need extra cash from bribes? The rubbish kept being churned out and I could take no more of it.

How could I motivate my team when I was feeling so besieged by these vile rumours? Some team-mates called me, knowing how depressed I was, but no official from the Pakistan Board of Control contacted me to express sympathy or support. Perhaps they felt there was some truth in the accusations. I hadn't felt totally supported by the board in recent months, and the chief executive Majid Khan appeared cool towards me. The lack of official support over the match-fixing allegations told me a lot. No one fought to change my mind when I told them I had to resign. I made it clear to the new captain, Rashid Latif, that I would give him all the help I could when we went on the tour to South Africa in February. It was more important to carry on playing for Pakistan than to be the captain.

I was clearly very naive about being picked for that tour. I was under the impression that I was still a good enough player, and the facts backed me up on that. Yet two weeks after I stood down as captain I was out in the cold, dropped from the tour party. There were no physical problems. The left shoulder which had had surgery six months earlier was fine, and I had proved my fitness by playing in a four-day match just before the selectors chose the tour squad. One of the selectors, Zaheer Abbas, made the point that I should not be dropped without evidence against me, but he was outvoted. It did not seem to matter that I was totally innocent of these outrageous charges of bribe taking.

After a few days spent licking my wounds in England, I resolved to make a fresh start, to rebuild my career. I would fight back. My cricket has been based on passion and full commitment, and no one is going to undermine me with these lies. I believe I have at least three good years left in me as a player at the highest level, and will strive to remain consistent. I will be the one who decides when I retire, not the gossip merchants. The warmth and sympathy I received from the Lancashire public when I flew in to launch my benefit year was very touching and gave me great strength. With my first season as county captain approaching, I saw silver linings amid the dark, traumatic clouds. I would throw myself into the job at Old Trafford, look forward to joining the boys on a fortnight's pre-season tour to Cape Town, and then show my capabilities as captain and player. The possibility of leading Lancashire to their first championship since 1934 excites me hugely and that sort of incentive will enable me to bounce back in a friendly and support-ive environment.

When I returned to Pakistan in February, I was still disillusioned about Pakistan cricket, although really positive about Lancashire and grateful to all at the club for their reassurances and support. Yet I couldn't let my omission from the South Africa tour rest, because it would appear that I was guilty of something. So I decided to go right to the top to get my name cleared. I asked for a meeting with the Prime Minister, Mian Nawaz Sharif, who I knew to be a great cricket fan, having played first-class cricket himself. The Prime Minister got my message asking for an urgent meeting, but he was just too busy to see me. Instead, he put me in touch with the Sports Minister, Sheik Rasheed, and over the next few days I had a number of high-powered meetings. I spoke to one of the speakers in the National Assembly, the equivalent to Parliament, and eventually I addressed a meeting of nine senators.

That's how important it was to me to get my name cleared. It was an exhausting process, going through all the accusations, rebutting them, getting the facts absolutely clear.

At the end of those meetings the senators and a judge ruled that there was no proof of corruption against me. No player should be dropped from the team unless accusations were proven. They ruled that selection should be based on performance and fitness, and nothing else – certainly not innuendo. The tribunal also requested that the press shouldn't harass any of the players looking for background because an inquiry was going to be set up. This inquiry would delve into all aspects of the corruption allegations that have dogged Pakistan cricket for so long. Every players involved in the various innuendos will be questioned by the senators. It will take time, but perhaps the slurs can at last be addressed. If players are guilty, then they must be punished, so that innocent ones like me can be judged to be untainted and free of suspicion.

Certainly the bandwagon to clean up Pakistan cricket is rolling with greater momentum after I had almost been sacrificed under the weight of all the innuendos. Throughout February, I was greatly helped by Khalid Mahmood, who had been appointed the new chairman of the Pakistan Cricket Board. He is a gentleman in the truest sense of the word who gave me a very fair hearing when I returned from England, feeling very bitter. He made it quite clear that he believed me, and that in the absence of contrary proof, I was innocent till proven guilty. Khalid Mahmood's persuasiveness won the day for me, and I was reinstated, selected for the last Test in South Africa and the Zimbabwe tour that followed. I went out there in a very positive frame of mind, eager to do well, convinced that I would eventually be totally exonerated. Inevitably, there was controversy about my reinstatement. The chairman of selectors, Salim Altaf resigned, saying my recall was in breach of the Board's constitution. Yet he was leaving the post anyway because he was to be transferred to Frankfurt by his employers, Pakistan International Airways.

All the players appeared happy and relieved when I turned up at Port Elizabeth at the start of March. Some of them even went out of their way to go public, telling the press they were delighted to have me there. I don't believe they ever doubted my innocence.

We've got to organise a situation where the whole mess is sorted out, so that players aren't left wondering why they're suddenly out of favour, and not picked for a tour they should be on. I believed Khalid Mahmood will play a pivotal role in these corruption investigations. He is an honest, straightforward man, and seems absolutely determined to stamp out all the rumours once and for all.

I just want to concentrate on my cricket now that I've been reinstated and I'm very happy to be playing under the captaincy of Rashid Latif. Yet it was significant that the Pakistan team which played in the Port Elizabeth Test in March 1998 contained six players who had captained our country. Having captained the side on two separate occasions, I wonder if I'll ever get a third chance? That doesn't concern me greatly. At least I'm back as a player, after being excluded for no real reason from the South African tour. My immediate priority as a captain is to win trophies for Lancashire, and as a Pakistan player, to clear my name for good. Then I can fully enjoy the rest of my career.

CHAPTER 2

Drifting into Cricket

IT NEVER occurred to me that cricket would become my career, let alone captaining my country. My only sporting ambition while at school was to be a top table tennis player. We didn't play cricket against other schools, and for a long time I thought nothing of an hour's cycle ride through the streets of Lahore for a game of table tennis. Yet by the time I was eighteen, I was playing cricket for Pakistan, with big names singing my praises. It was bewildering. I had come from nowhere, with barely an idea about the skills and tactics involved in playing top-class cricket. It could only happen in India or Pakistan, where the game is played by so many, with the vast majority falling by the wayside through lack of opportunity, money or encouragement. I was so lucky to have everything flowing in my favour. All I did to get noticed was to be in the right place at the right time, impressing some influential people. The hard work, building on my good fortune, would come later.

I came from a prosperous background, probably upper middle class in English social terms, so as boy I never had to worry about leaving school early to earn some money for my family. My father's spare parts business was successful enough to allow us to live in the comfortable suburb of Modeltown in Lahore and his three sons – Naeem, Nadeem and myself – and daughter Sofia didn't have to wear the same clothes, day after day. My parents were strict, though, and they made sure I attended a good school, the Cathedral School in Lahore. I was expected to do something worthwhile with my professional life after my education was completed, but for now my parents were happy to send me to a fee-paying school, where discipline and respect for elders were major considerations.

Fortunately, English was spoken and taught at this school, and for that I have always been grateful. When I see teenagers coming into the senior Pakistan side unable to grasp what English-speaking journalists or opponents are saying, I realise with relief how fortunate I was that my place of learning was modelled on a British school. I shall always be a proud Pakistani, with Urdu my first language, but being able to speak English and to understand and appreciate English humour has certainly helped me get along with people from other countries. I'm sure it was a decisive factor when I first played for Lancashire at the age of twenty-two as I had to come to terms quickly with a totally different lifestyle and dressing-room atmosphere.

Cricket was hugely popular in Lahore when I was growing up, partly because the Pakistan national side was beginning to make an impact on the world game, with so many great players coming through. Just like any sports-mad youngster, I was proud to hear about the exploits of Zaheer Abbas, Sarfraz Nawaz, Javed Miandad and Imran Khan. If anyone had told me that within a few years I'd be playing alongside such heroes and benefiting from their advice, I would have laughed. I still wanted to be a top table tennis player; I was tall and skinny, with a long reach at the table and quick reactions. Cricket for me was only an enjoyable way of passing the time.

When I was about ten, I went to live with my grandparents because they were just five minutes away from school. There was nothing traumatic about that, it's common arrangement among Pakistan families, and I loved living with my grandparents, as did my sister Sofia who went to the same school. We lived there for about ten years, but I still saw my parents, who would drive over from Modeltown, nearly every day. That change of address brought me closer to cricket, though. My grandfather loved the game. He used to listen to the radio commentaries, telling me about the deeds of Zaheer and the others. I started to play in the narrow streets near their home in Old Lahore and I found it great fun. Day after day, night after night, we'd be in the streets with a soft ball and a set of stumps, with the houses, almost touching each other across the street, standing witness to our tense matches. We'd set up a tournament with as many as ten teams involved, each paying an entrance fee and the winners scooping the pool. Extra pocket money was always welcome! The cricket was very competitive and fast, testing out the quality of your reactions and eyesight. Whenever a rickshaw came down the street, we'd pick up the stumps, then start over again. You had to get used to ricochets coming at you from all angles, and sometimes things got rather too heated and passionate – sounds like almost every Pakistan team I've played for!

I was hooked. Table tennis started to take a back seat, with my grandmother conniving in my increasing love for cricket. My parents were very strict about homework, but my grandmother used to say, 'Go to cricket, but don't tell your mother,' and she'd handle all that as I enjoyed myself. I had enough money to be able to afford to buy a bat from England – it was a Stuart Surridge – but I broke it after just two days' use. Trading it in for two Pakistan bats seemed a good idea at the time, and I certainly got my money's worth out of the deal. Today, my beloved grandmother is almost blind, but still mentally sharp. Whenever I go to see her, she hugs me tightly and says, 'You're very clever.' That makes me very proud, because she spoiled me terribly and loved me dearly. Without that bright light of encouragement from my grandparents, I doubt if I would have been interested enough in the game which has given me so much.

Again, I was lucky in my decision to go to a coaching camp organised by my school. It seemed a far better idea than studying for exams, so I went along. After all, cricket was a lot of fun in the streets, so it was worth giving it a try on matting. We played six-overs-a-side matches, I bowled leg spin with an occasional fast spell, and when I batted I spent all my time at the crease trying to hit sixes. (Not a lot has changed in that department!) Anyway, I must have been doing something right during those carefree games, because I was singled out by someone who knew about first-class cricket. Khalid Mahmood had played for Pakistan Customs against many of Pakistan's top players, and he came up to me and said:

'You've got something, you could be a cricketer.' Of course, I didn't believe him – you don't do you? One minute your're tearing around in the middle with your mates, trying to hit the ball out of the ground, and then a respectable man with a lot of cricketing knowledge and practical experience is telling you that you could make something of yourself. No one had ever been that encouraging with my table tennis, so I saw no harm in taking up his offer to join his club, Ludhiana Gymkhana. Khalid clearly saw potential in me because he used to take me to matches on his bicycle, with me squashed up at the front, travelling miles to play cricket. I was only sixteen. Two years later, I was playing in a Test match.

Around that time, I left school and went to Islamia College to study Fine Arts. Sounds impressive, but I mustn't delude anybody. I was no academic, and the only studying I did around that time was in the cricket nets and during matches. I was doing well at Ludhiana, with Khalid Mahmood teaching me how to bowl fast, telling me that I had the raw ability to succeed at the top, that being left-handed was a bonus because batsmen aren't comfortable with left-hand bowlers. I was in no position to know whether or not he was telling the truth, but it was nice to be encouraged, especially so because Zahid Khan, who also played for Ludhiana and was the captain of our college side, wouldn't pick me for Islamia. He'd say: 'We've got senior players in their last year who have priority over you. Next year, you'll play regularly.' So for a season I was twelfth man for my college side. I never did get a game for them, and six months after leaving Islamia College I was in the Pakistan eleven. My college captain was a good judge, wasn't he?!

By the time I was eighteen, I was living and breathing cricket. I'd read and heard all about Pakistan's stirring exploits under the captaincy of the glamorous Imran Khan, particularly on the tour to England in 1982 when Pakistan appeared unlucky to lose the series. I'd been in the crowd for the Lahore Test in March 1984, watching Abdul Qadir take ten wickets in the match, enjoying David Gower's unbeaten hundred for England, and rejoicing that the draw had brought a series victory for Pakistan. In common with all Pakistanis, I had reacted enviously to India winning the World Cup the year before, beating West Indies in the final. One day, I hoped, our country would lift that trophy. I didn't allow myself the luxury of thinking that I'd have any part to play in that, but I was happy to be swept along by waves of outrageous luck in that year of 1984.

One day, my club played Lahore Gymkhana, and in that side were the noted Test players Ramiz Raja and Intikhab Alam. I bowled quickly, took four wickets, and several good judges started talking about me. At that time, the best hundred young players in the Lahore area were sent to summer camp to have their abilities dissected and assessed by top-class coaches, with the aim of pushing through quickly the most obvious talent. This was promoted by the Pakistan Board of Control and taken very seriously by all concerned, because the board had made it clear that, with cricket becoming more popular in Pakistan, young talent had to be nurtured and blooded speedily. The board, the equivalent to England's Test and County Cricket Board at the time, was charged with the overall responsibility of running cricket in Pakistan. After my performance against Lahore Gymkhana, I was chosen for that summer camp, and even a naive youngster like me realised then that it had been a good time to impress Ramiz and Intikhab.

The first month of the camp was held on home territory for me, the Gaddafi Stadium in Lahore, and the coach in charge was clearly impressed with me. Agha Saadat had played for Pakistan thirty years earlier during our country's early period in Test cricket, and so I assumed he knew a lot about the game. When he started to take a great interest in my bowling, I was thrilled. By this time, the flickering competitive instinct that had been fanned by those back-street matches outside my grandparents' home was buring strongly. I was going to make the second month of that summer camp; I couldn't cope with the disappointment of rejection. I knew nothing about the game's finer points, but felt there was something there to build on. Certainly the experienced coaches thought so. I was itching to improve.

They did pick me for the second month, and again word-of-mouth worked in my favour. Agha Saadat had talked about me to Khan Mohammad, a former fast bowler who had represented Pakistan several times twenty years earlier, and an influential adviser to the selectors. He came along to the nets that second month and worked on my action. I had no idea about the mechanics of fast bowling, I just ran up and let the ball go as fast as possible, but Khan Mohammed was very patient with the rawest of raw material. He made me get more sideways on in my action, telling me that was the way to swing the ball, and he worked on getting my bowling arm up higher, to generate extra bounce. He also told me that I'd be even quicker if I cocked my left arm as I was in my delivery stride, giving an extra thrust to my momentum. It all sounded very technical, but the way he explained and demonstrated it was very straightforward. Happily, he had no desire to tame my wildness at that stage, just to build on what he saw as my natural talent.

I was desperate to succeed at that second camp. It was held in Karachi, and my father showed his support by buying me a plane ticket so that I wouldn't be exhausted by a train journey. Few at that camp could have afforded such a luxury, and that only made me even more determined to make everything count. Among those at the Karachi camp were Ramiz Raja, Mohsin Kamal – both of whom had made their Test debuts a few months earlier against England – and Ijaz Ahmed, who was to become a top batsman for Pakistan, so the competition was fierce.

I had a huge boost to my confidence when Agha Saadat gave me the new ball. Even then I realised how important that was in the dry, dusty conditions. The only chance you had to swing the ball was early on, before the ball got soft and worn down by the impact of the bat and its travels over the bumpy outfield, clattering against the boundary boards. I'd bowl three hours on the trot, never giving away that precious new ball, and whenever the coaches enquired if I needed a rest, I'd reassure them I was fine. I'm sure I didn't look it – I was still tall and gangly, with no muscles – but I just kept going in the heat. At various stages, I got all the best players out, including Ramiz and Ijaz, and I enjoyed the rivalry between us. I was discovering a fierce desire for competition I didn't know I had in me, and my ambition was surging at the same time.

Again, I got lucky. The chief selector of the national side at the time, Haseeb Hassan, happened to be at the stadium one day when I was bowling particularly well at the star batsmen, and I understand he noted down my name, with Agha Saadat and Khan

Mohammad pressing my claims. When the camp finished, Khan Mohammad told the local press that I had the potential to play for Pakistan, that I was genuinely fast and definitely one for the future. I was overwhelmed. It seemed only months ago that I'd preferred table tennis and played cricket in the streets till it was dark and my grandmother was calling me in to go to bed. Now there was a glimmer of a chance that I could make a career of cricket. The praise of Khan Mohammad had inspired me to the extent that if I failed to make the grade it wouldn't be through lack of dedication. At the age of eighteen, I had a purpose in life.

So I set to work on my bowling in the nets at the Ludhiana Gymkhana. At the time, my batting was an afterthought. Nobody had coached me on batting at that stage, and I batted number eleven for every team I played for, so I was under no illusions about that part of my game. It was much more vital to remember the advice of my coaches when bowling, to get used to bowling from a side-on position, and to keep my left arm up high. Then one day I happened to glance at a newspaper and, turning to the sports pages, I had the shock of my life: I had been selected to play against the touring New Zealand side. That's how I found out about my debut in first-class cricket, a debut that was to place me in the record books. My name was in the squad for the Pakistan Board XI to play the New Zealanders in Rawalpindi; I was going to compete with the likes of John Wright, Martin Crowe and Lance Cairns. The captain of our team was no less a cricketer than Javed Miandad, and he'd be leading out players like Shoaib Mohammad, Ramiz Raja and Salim Malik, three batsmen I'd watched in the Lahore Test against England eight months earlier. This match was also scheduled to be shown on television. I was flabbergasted, but elated.

Eventually, reality seeped into me and I came into to the conclusion that I was only going to Rawalpindi for the ride, to get some practical experience, watching the first eleven at close quarters, drinking in the atmosphere. After all, I was only in the squad; there was no suggestion that I would be playing. We flew together to Pindi and I found it a tremendous adventure just being with the team. My heart was bursting with pride. The night before the start, Javed Miandad took me to one side, said I was playing, wished me luck, and that was it. It took some time for it all to sink in and then I started to get very nervous. I had only a basic grasp of fast bowling at that stage and had no idea what plans I should make to bowl at world-class batsmen like Wright and Crowe. And the match was to be live on television! This could be the end of my dreams, with my bowling being smashed all over the stadium. I certainly didn't communicate my fears to my team-mates (I was very naive at eighteen, but not that naive!), but four of us who were about the same age and sharing two rooms agreed that whoever did well would buy a big dinner.

One night later, we were having roast dinner together and I was footing the bill. I had no complaints because I had taken seven wickets. On my first-class debut! Against Test batsmen! Even now I find it hard to credit the events of that first day in Rawalpindi. I've since got used to the fact that in Pakistan, players seem to spring up overnight from obscurity to make a major impact on the stage. We do seem to be more precocious compared to cricketers in England, where promising young talent often appears to be held back, but at the age of eighteen I didn't know about our national philosophy, which, broadly speaking, can be summarised as 'throw them in early, and see if they can swim'. I also didn't know until later that my captain, Javed Miandad, had gone out on a limb for me. During that second month's camp in his home city of Karachi a few months earlier, Javid had come into the stadium for a net. It seems I caught his eye and he talked about me to the coaches. So *he* was behind my selection for the game at Rawalpindi. He then insisted that I played, selecting me ahead of a Test bowler, Tahir Naqqash, who had toured all over the world with Pakistan in the early eighties. Can you imagine that happening in another country, an eighteen-year-old selected ahead of a Test bowler on the basis of one session in the nets? It's something I kept in my mind when I became captain of Pakistan. You must give youth its chance, even if it means alienating another, older player. Imran Khan had the same attitude when he was the captain, and I was one of the many beneficiaries of his philosophy.

On that first morning at Rawalpindi I was glad to get the chance to bowl straight away, to deal with my nerves. Around ten thousand people were there for the first game of the New Zealand tour, and as I ran in to bowl I tried hard to keep out of my mind the fact that the television cameras were on me. There was a great strategy, I just ran up with the shiny side of the ball facing the batsman. This meant that the ball hopefully would come in to the left-hand batsmen, with three of them in the first five in their order. All I tried to do was get the ball down to the other end as quickly and as straight as I could, hoping that its newness would make it swing for me. It did, and I got John Wright caught in the slips early on. That settled me down. My team-mates were very encouraging, and as the ball got older, it seemed to swing late for me. I cleaned up the tail, taking the last four wickets and ending up with 7 for 50 in 20.5 overs. So I hadn't even been expensive, as well as dismissing batsmen who had made Test hundreds. I was absolutely thrilled, delighted that the match had been televised, and I rang my parents in Lahore to check if they'd been watching. Of course they had, and they were very proud. Never has roast chicken on hotel room service tasted so good!

After taking another two wickets in the second innings, I was Pakistan's latest overnight sensation. The first of the one-day internationals was just two days away, but I wasn't picked. Perhaps I'd make it for the Test a week later? After all, Sarfraz Nawaz had announced his retirement after that first one-dayer, so wasn't there now room for the latest young blood? The arrogance of youth! I had temporarily forgotten that just eight months had elapsed between my watching a Test and expecting to appear in one, in the meantime having played just three days of first-class cricket. It was deservedly a rude awakening for me, just what I needed to take me down a peg or two.

A fortnight after my debut at Rawalpindi, I played in the one-day international at Faisalabad and found out the hard way how little I really knew about the game of cricket. In a rain-interrupted match, the overs were reduced to twenty per side and the New Zealanders were left to get seven an over. My captain, the great Zaheer Abbas, gave me the final over, with a win for us seemingly a formality. They needed twenty-four to win only three wickets in hand, and Zaheer obviously thought it was a good time to give his debutant fast bowler practical experience of bowling at the end of an innings, when the slog was on. It nearly backfired, because they ended up just five runs short, with Jeremy Coney hitting me for six-teen off four balls with four boundaries in a row. I made the mis-take of bowling too short on what was a green wicket, and Coney punished my lack of direction. The situation cried out for a reduc-tion in pace and a pitching up of the ball, but I was too carried away with trying to knock Coney's head off. One of the fielders said to me, 'Bowl him a yorker,' but I had no idea what he was talking about. Nobody had yet instructed me how to bowl a yorker, a delivery that became one of my specialities, squeezing a ball of full length under the bat and beating the player with speed and late swing. I had never even heard of the word 'yorker', I was that raw. So we scraped home, and although team-mates such as Mudassar Nazar, Mohsin Khan and Javed Miandad were support-ive afterwards, my captain didn't say a word to me. I thought Zaheer might have sat me down and talked through that final over with me, asking what I was trying to do, but he didn't. He was one of my idols, so I didn't feel it was right for a young kid to approach the master, and I was disappointed that he appeared unconcerned about my morale, which had obviously plummeted in the space of one over. That incident is something I keep in mind when a young player plays for Pakistan under my captaincy.

I wasn't picked again to face the New Zealanders, either in the remaining two Tests or one-dayers. Had I blown my chances? It wouldn't be the first time a young Pakistani player had been fast-tracked by influential seniors, only to be case aside after one bad game. Yet I was determined now, I wanted to give my all to be part of my country's cricketing future. I took up an invitation to move to Karachi, to play in a higher standard of cricket, representing Pakistan Automobiles. I earned about twenty pounds a month, but that didn't matter because all I did was sleep and play cricket, day after day. I lived cheaply in a hostel, and spent every available hour either in the nets or out in the middle. My parents were very sup-portive, I phoned them regularly, and I think they were pleased that at last I found something to fire my energies and imagination. That fleeting, elusive taste of the big time, playing for my country in front of 20,000 fanatical supporters, stayed in my memory and drove me on. Faisalabad wasn't going to be the only ground where I represented Pakistan. I wanted to play Test cricket.

A month after Faisalabad, I was summoned to the training camp that always precedes a Pakistan tour or international series. The coaches and selectors like to get the players on their own, work them hard without any distractions, check out fitness levels, and assess which of the promising youngsters is worthy of promotion. I was so happy for myself and my family that I was included in that party of twenty-five players. In a few weeks, Pakistan would be touring New Zealand, and places were up for grabs. I was bursting with enthusiasm, determined to bowl well in the nets at our top batsmen. Luckily, I seemed to reserve my best for Javed Miandad, who was not only one of the world's best batsmen, but also the captain of the tour party. I know I impressed him, but didn't realise how much. He struck his neck out for me, demanding that I had to be picked for the tour. Apparently, some of the selectors believed I was too raw (I wouldn't have argued with that), but Javed dug his heels in. At one stage, he said that if Wasim Akram wasn't picked, then he wouldn't be going either. I would learn in later years the true extent of Javed Miandad's stubborness – to my cost at times, when I was captain – but his obstinacy worked in my favour in December 1984. He was backed up by the chairman of selectors, Haseeb Hassan, another of my supporters, and I got the vote.

Just a few months after leaving Islamia College, deciding a Fine Arts degree wasn't a major ambition, I was off to New Zealand to represent my country. At eighteen years of age, after just one game of first-class cricket. All this without any representative tour or under-19 international to see if I had the potential. In Pakistan, you have a great start if a few influential people rate you. In my case, it was Javed Miandad when he was going through one of his periods as captain. You can't get much luckier than that. I know everyone needs luck to get a start in life, but at such an early stage in my career I had enjoyed bucketfuls of the stuff. A lot of people had put their faith in me, and I would be working flat out to repay them.

CHAPTER 3

In at the Deep End

I WAS so naive when I went on my first Pakistan tour. It was marvellous to hear how Javed Miandad had gone into bat for me to get me on that tour to New Zealand, and when I heard that I'd also be going on to Australia afterwards to play in a one-day series of matches, I was overjoyed. Before leaving for New Zealand, I rang up my captain to ask how much money I'd need to take on the tour. Javed laughed out loud and said, 'Don't be silly, you get a daily allowance!' An allowance for playing for your country? That was amazing to me; I was quite prepared to pay for all expenses out of my own pocket. I had a lot to learn. Over the next two years my passport was stamped by customs officials all over the world, as my cricketing education in a hectic round of series and tours: Jan/Feb 1985 to New Zealand; Feb/March to Australia; March to Sharjah; Oct/Nov to Sri Lanka; Nov to Sharjah; Nov/Dec at home to West Indies; Feb/April 1986 to Sri Lanka; April to Sharjah; May/Sept to England to play league cricket; Oct/Nov at home to West Indies; Nov/Dec to Sharjah; Dec/Jan 1987 to Australia; Jan/March to India; April to Sharjah. So, in just over two years I had played Tests and one-day Internationals on ten official tours, as well as getting used to English conditions for a summer.

By the time I arrived in England for our full tour in May 1987, I had learned an enormous amount about top-class cricket, and I was still a month away from my twenty-first birthday. Thanks to fantastic advice from several experienced Pakistan colleagues, I was almost the finished product as a fast bowler by the time that tour to England began. Of course, there was any amount of fine tuning needed and hard work ahead to instil the disciplines so that I could automatically reproduce what had been drummed into me, but it was a major head start compared to other fast bowlers of the same age from other countries. An English bowler, in particular, would probably still be on the fringes of his country's first team at a similar age, whereas I had enjoyed the privilege of learning my trade at the highest level by practical experience. You can't show your true capabilities just bowling in the nets, or getting an occasional innings against weak opposition. It's positive attitude to youth that has served Pakistan well in my time in the side.

That crowded two years of my life was a wonderful experience, and not just in cricketing teams. Touring helped to rid me of unworldliness and innocence, and toughened me up. That first tour to New Zealand was an eye-opener. I remember being so excited at being in a plane that was going to take almost a day to fly to New Zealand. The senior players just wanted to sleep, but I chattered away. Javed Miandad even gave me his food to keep me quiet! Our manager, Yawar Saeed, was so understanding towards me, smiling at my wide-eyed enthusiasm and giving me sound advice throughout the tour. I even went to my first nightclub with some of the boys, the strobe lighting was dazzling, and the music very loud, but the atmosphere was fantastic, a completely new experience for me. And to think we also had a daily allowance!

Despite the social distractions, there was no way I was going to fail through a lack of effort. As soon as we landed in Christchurch, at four in the morning, I went for a jog, and the first net practice couldn't come too quickly for me. I was simply bursting with pleasure and excitement at being on my first tour, alongside players who had been idols to me. Going straight into the Test side was an ambition, of course, but I kept that bottled up, hoping I'd make a good early impression. I was picked for the three-day game against Canterbury at Christchurch, but didn't take a wicket in twenty-nine overs. I also split open my hand in the field, and it needed four stitches, so I was pretty dispirited by the end of that game. The first couple of one-day internationals came and went without me, and then I wasn't picked for the First Test at Wellington. The irony was that the fast bowler picked ahead of me was Tahir Naqqash, the unlucky one who had had to stand down for me the previous November at Javed Miandad's insistence, which led to my first-class debut and nine wickets in the match. Tahir Naqqash wouldn't have been human if he hadn't been inwardly happy at seeing off my early challenge on the New Zealand tour. Hopefully, I'd get my chance at some stage. I had told myself that I wasn't coming on this tour as a reserve, or to be categorised as just a one-day player. I wanted to be a genuine, respected Test cricketer – as soon as possible.

The second Test was played just a few days later in Auckland, and I made it. Not with any great fanfare, though. I went to bed the night before convinced the team wouldn't be changing, but Javed looked at the green wicket next morning, decided to drop one of our spinners, and came over to me to say, 'You're playing.' You might have thought I'd be exhilarated, but in all honesty I started to panic. Watching the previous Test, it had really come home to me how much hard work was involved in Test cricket, especially bowling on slow surfaces like the ones in New Zealand. Now I was going to play, and all sorts of negative thoughts started to fly around my head. I had never bowled more than an eight-over spell in senior cricket, let alone keep one end going for the best part of a Test session. Where would I find the stamina to bowl for five days in a row at batsmen of the calibre of Martin Crowe, Geoff Howarth, Jeremy Coney and John Wright? How would I cope with batting against the great Richard Hadlee? I soon had the answer to that one: Hadlee had me caught at short leg for nought. He had already hit me on the shin, and because I was wearing very thin pads, the blow had hurt. I had prayed to get just a single to avoid a duck on my debut, but he overwhelmed me. On top of that, my shin was very sore. How could I bowl now?

Next day I opened the bowling but fared badly on a green wicket that ought to have suited me. My leg hurt and I struggled against the experienced Howarth and Wright. In my second spell, I did manage to get my first Test wicket – Wright caught in the gully – and I gave thanks to my God after praying that I could bowl better. Towards the end of the New Zealand innings, with the slogging on just before the declaration, I dismissed Ian Smith to finish with

2 for 105. It was a disappointing effort by me and the other bowlers, and we were demoralised. They bowled us out cheaply on the fourth day to win by an innings. It was a harsh introduction to Test cricket.

Would I now be sidelined for the rest of the tour? Was it time for Javed Miandad to revert to his senior fast bowlers? That was certainly the case for the next three-day game against Wellington, and the following one-day international in Christchurch. It looked as if I was going to miss out for the last Test, a game I needed to play in to raise my spirits. I was working hard in the nets, still as keen as ever, but I knew that many a young Pakistani cricketer has been picked out of the blue for a tour, then abruptly dumped back into oblivion when it was over. That second chance was vital for me.

That chance came, courtesy of the Dunedin weather. It had rained a fair amount, and Javed decided to play no spinners and go in with four seamers on another green pitch, I hadn't expected to play, and when I got the tap on my shoulder I soon got myself into a positive frame of mind. I was determined this time not to be over-awed, to look the opposition straight in the eye and not back down. This game I'd be looking to bowl maidens, rather than try to blast them out in conditions that should favour me. They certainly did. I made history: the youngest player to take ten wickets in a Test. For the record, I bowled fifty-eight overs in the match, taking 10 for 128, five in each innings. And we lost. That was the only black spot in a memorable five days for me, but it was the worst moment of all, especially as I felt responsible to a large extent. When I needed to take the wicket of a tail-ender to win the game, I was found wanting, lacking mental strength. That allowed New Zealand to come out on top in a match they should have lost.

Javed and Mudassar Nazar had worked hard in the nets with me after my disappointing Test debut, telling me what batsmen don't like from fast bowlers, and they both drummed into me the need for accuracy in conditions that suit me. I had to develop patience, prey on batsmen's nerves, wait for the mistakes. It worked a treat in Dunedin, but I wouldn't have made it without the advice of those two experienced team-mates. One of them was always stationed at mid-off when I walked back, repeating the mental disciplines I needed. So I just pitched the ball up, hoped for the best on a wicket of uneven bounce, and went into the history books. That sounds a bit simplistic, I know, but that's really all there was to it. There was no repertoire of different deliveries to call on at that stage of my career – I was so raw and unsophisticated technically – so I just put the ball there or thereabouts and it misbehaved at regular intervals, taking off or shooting through low.

On the face of it, mine would have been a matchwinning performance in any other Test match, except that Jeremy Coney had other ideas. Having already suffered at his hands on my one-day debut a few months earlier, I knew what a fierce competitor he was, and he proved it here with a great effort to win the Test from a desperate position. New Zealand needed 278 to win, the highest score of the game, with the pitch deteriorating. I managed to fire out their first four batsmen to leave them 23 for 4, yet they still won it, with the ball moving sideways and leaping off a length. At one stage we had them 228 for 8, in effect for 9 because I had put Lance Cairns in hospital. He had come in without a helmet, and that was enough to make me lose my focus and start bowling bouncers at him. I hit him on the back of the head, and he went down, concussed. He was taken to hospital, where he spent the next three days. I visited him after the game and he told me it was an accident, that I shouldn't worry about it and that he ought to have worn a helmet on a wicket of such uneven bounce.

All that was in the future though, and after Cairns was led away, I lost control. The last man, Ewen Chatfield, wasn't much of a batsman, and the plan was to bounce him out, leaving Coney stranded. It didn't work. I bowled too wide and too short, picking up an official warning for persistent use of the short-pitched delivery. In retrospect, that was fair enough. I ought to have had more in my technical armoury to blow Chatfield away legitimately, but I was too fired up, not thinking clearly enough. Chatfield batted very bravely, picking up many bruises, but he held firm and Coney won the game for New Zealand with a gutsy unbeaten century. As I had dropped New Zealand's matchwinner on thirty-seven – an easy caught and bowled – I found it hard to be too generous towards him, but I soon learned to appreciate what he had done for his side.

After the game, I did my first television interview. It was a nerve-racking experience, and although the interviewer was full of praise for my ten wickets, I knew I should have won the game for Pakistan. That Test made me realise just how hard a game it is at the top level, because I allowed myself to be distracted by injuring Lance Cairns when, by his own admission, it was his fault. Helmets at that time were already widely used, so why not put one on when the ball is taking off? Dunedin 1984 was a landmark for me. I was now a Test record-holder, but the defeat toughened me up, made me more competitive. It made me realise that the team's success is everything, that top-class sport is not just about sparkling individual contributions. That sort of awareness can only come through bitter experience.

There wasn't a great deal of time to mull over the deep disappointment of my first Test loss because we were soon off to Australia to play in the World Championship of Cricket, organised by Benson and Hedges and featuring all seven Test countries. For me it was a fantastic experience, playing against some of the world's greats, under lights for the first time in my life. The new lights at the Melbourne Cricket Ground were used for the first time in this tournament, and more than 82,000 were there for the first match, Australia against England. It was a wonderful time to be a young player just starting off in international cricket. The crowds were enthusiastic, the facilities superb, and the atmosphere of night cricket was unbelievable, so inspirational. The MCG has always inspired me, especially in a day/night match, and it was no fluke that I managed to help Pakistan win the World Cup at the MCG seven years later. If you've got any pride in your performance, you can't help turning it on there.

On that first trip to Australia I got into the action straight away, getting the man of the match award when we beat the home side. I took 5 for 21 to reduce them to 42 for 5, but I must give some of the credit to the player who became my biggest supporter and greatest mentor, Imran Khan. He had joined us for this tour from a period of convalescence in Australia after his shin splints operation, an injury that had troubled him for a couple of years. I had never met him, and when he came over to introduce himself, I was tongue-tied. 'Well done,' he said. 'You bowled very well in New Zealand.' My heart was huge; my idol was congratulating me, treating me with respect. I soon realised that he genuinely rated me.

Although Javed Miandad was still the captain, Imran took me under his wing and stood at mid-off whenever I bowled, ready with advice. When I started to get among the Australian wickets during that game at Melbourne, Imran told me what to do when Kim Hughes walked in. 'Bowl him a bouncer,' he commanded, 'he won't be able to resist it.' Sure enough, Hughes misjudged the pull to the first bouncer I sent down and was caught at mid-on for a single. That was the first practical example of Imran's insight and strong belief in players whom he rated in his side. It was a characteristic that I admired greatly over the years, as he spent so much time generously with me, smoothing out the rough edges.

He was there for me again later in that series against England when I bowled badly at Allan Lamb and David Gower, going for six an over. He and Javed reassured me, saying that the English batsmen had played well, but I was concerned that I couldn't seem to do much when the ball wasn't swinging. Imran said, 'Don't worry, we'll teach you the slower ball, and where to aim for when the batsmen are on the slog. You can't get five wickets all the time. Learn patience and discipline.' See what I mean about luck? It had been memorable enough so far to have a great player like Javed Miandad telling me what to look out for in a batsman, but now I had one of the world's great fast bowlers giving me the benefit of his vast experience, willingly and relevantly. Who couldn't improve in that sort of company?

After that marvellous first taste of cricket in Australia, we were whisked off to Sharjah for a one-day series involving England, Australia, India and Pakistan. This was the first time the sides had been chosen by their respective boards of control, an indication that the prestige and stature of the Sharjah tournament was about to soar. I was lucky to be in at the start of the growth of cricket in Sharjah, and I know that playing on those slow wickets has helped my all-round game. The crowds were partisan on my first trip, especially when India and Pakistan played each other, and each game was very competitive. That was the start of a great relationship between myself and the Sharjah Trophy, and our two trips a year have benefited Pakistan circket handsomely.

By April 1985 it was time for a breather. It had been an amazing experience for me, packed full of moments that would make me a better cricketer. I had bowled at Martin Crowe, Allan Border, Dean Jones, Sunil Gavaskar, Viv Richards, Clive Lloyd, Desmond Haynes, Kapil Dev and David Gower. Imran Khan had put his arm around me, making it clear I had enough talent to gain his respect. That alone would have been enough satisfaction if I had never played another game of cricket. As I turned nineteen, my life had changed completely. I was now fiercely ambitious, deeply proud to represent my country. The increased public attention didn't bother me at all, in fact I lapped it up. It was great to see my name in the newspapers, to be asked for interviews for television, to be aware that cricket fans back home would be watching me on TV, running in to bowl. Forgive me the arrogance of youth. I would eventually learn who to trust in the media after being hurt by all sorts of damaging accusations, but when you're only just nineteen and you're doing well in international sport, it's only human nature to lap up all the praise. All my family were so happy for me, that I was achieving something on their behalf, and my gran was more delighted than anybody after those years encouraging me to skip homework and play cricket instead outside her home!

The good things in life started to flow. With various tour fees now coming in regularly, I bought my first car, a Toyota Corolla, and I opened a bank account for the first time. But I didn't rest on my laurels, apart from a three-week holiday. There was much work to do, especially honing and developing my bowling technique and building up my stamina and physique. I was still too skinny, my legs had to be stronger for the hard work ahead. Imran had told me what was necessary for a fast bowler to last the pace, and back home in Lahore I found someone who encouraged me totally in my fitness campaign. Saud Khan had played first-class cricket for United Bank and he was marvellous to me when I needed strong direction. I'd wake up at five every morning, go for a run, then Saud would pick me up, take me to the ground, and work me very hard. He intoduced me to physical training – stretching and sprinting for explosive flexibility, and long runs for stamina. Then he'd supervise me in two long net sessions daily.

I almost lived at the ground, spending about seven hours there every day. Training, netting and fielding – that was the unchanging routine. I could eat anything I wanted, because it was agreed I needed fattening up. Sounds monotonous, but it wasn't, because I could see the purpose of it all. It was simply a case of building on what I'd already started to do earlier in the year in New Zealand and Australia. Even when I wasn't playing I'd run five laps of the ground, then warm down with some stretching routines. The importance of a fast bowler having good legs wasn't lost on me, even when I was making my first wide-eyed tour. Perhaps it was that sort of awareness which impressed Imran and prompted him to back me so enthusiastically. I hope so, because there really are no short-cuts in international cricket.

Imran was now back as Pakistan's captain, and in case anyone thought he was being unduly biased towards me, he kept me out of the one-day series against our next opponents, Sri Lanka. I was very down that I didn't even get one outing in the four games, but I never found out why. You didn't ask Imran Khan such questions, especially when you've just turned nineteen. He chose me, though, for the three Tests against Sri Lanka, and he and I opened the bowling, but I didn't impress. Clearly my captain felt I needed more technical guidance, because he and Mudassar Nazar put in a lot of time with me in the nets around that period. They talked to me about reverse swing – where the ball moves the opposite way to where it's expected to go – and they indoctrinated me with the disciplines needed to make the ball swing in either orthodox or unorthodox fashion. For reverse swing to the right-hander they told me to hold the shiny side towards the batsman, to hold it on the outside for the outswinger, and to make sure that the rough side is kept dry so that it will move in the air late. They didn't know why such things affected the ball's behaviour any more than I did. It is a case of aerodynamics, I suppose, but the mathematics are too complicated for cricketers.

During the match, Imran would stand alongside me as I walked back to my mark and outline how he felt the over should be constructed. 'Inswinger, outswinger, good length ball, bouncer if he doesn't fancy it. Keep your head still and line up where you want to pitch the ball. If you want an inswinger, aim at first slip, and the ball will end up around middle and off stump.' Usually, he was dead right. I was in awe of his technical ability and his solid belief in me. I am forever in his debt.

When we toured Sri Lanka in the early part of 1986, Imran gave me another invaluable lesson. In a one-dayer at Kandy, Asantha de Mel slogged me for sixteen in my last over, damaging runs to concede at that stage of the innings. I had bowled too short. Afterwards, Imran told me I had to learn how to bowl the yorker at will, not just now and again. I needed to be able to rely on producing it whenever necessary, especially when the opposition was throwing the bat. I asked him how to learn it and he took me into the nets. 'Put just one off-stump up and aim at the top of it,' he told me, and I hit the stump's base four times in the three overs I bowled in front of him. When he left me to practise it , I got more and more consistent. In the next one-dayer, at Coloumbo, I took 4 for 28, three of them with yorkers, including the wicket of de Mel. That ability to bowl the yorker has stayed with me ever since that net session with Imran. You can't beat such practical tuition when you're so young. Imran told me that you need pace for the yorker to get it under the bat; it had to be an 'effort' ball. To get reverse swing, it was also vital to deliver it at speed. Apparently the rough side of the ball reacts favourably in relation to air currents if it is travelling quickly rather than curving at medium pace. So if I could manage to generate speed and accuracy, I had a chance of getting batsmen with the inswinger when they were expecting the outswinger.

The potential for wicket-taking when you have embraced such knowledge is so much greater. You see so many batsmen shoulder arms to a ball they believe is passing outside off-stump, particularly at Test level where you're not expected to be playing at every delivery, looking for runs. So if you can deceive them with one that dips in late, the chances of getting them out lbw, playing no stroke, or clean bowling them with a dipping, late yorker are so much greater. Learning those skills was a breakthrough for my bowling, a giant leap forward from being a quick but raw tearaway to a dangerous swing bowler with the ability to generate late swing at speed. That was particularly important: Imran told me that Test batsmen have keen eyesight and good reactions, so if they see the ball swing early enough, they can make adjustments. The art was to maintain high pace while getting them to play in the wrong areas.

Such a bowling technique was obviously worth trying to master, so I started to carry around a ball that was around forty overs old and I worked with it on reverse swing whenever I was in the nets. Imran said that a ball forty to fifty overs old was ideal to generate reverse swing, because there was still enough shine available on one side, but the ball generally would be getting worn. The tactic was to keep the rough side as dry as possible. When I worked on this in the nets, it seemed to do what Imran had forecast, so I kept practising the same way month after month, all over the world, in various nets. Years later, when reverse swing became the exciting new cricket tactic, I was very grateful for Imran's guidance which had inspired me to work so hard at a bowling style that can trouble even the world's best batsmen when the conditions are favourable.

Imran hadn't finished with me, though. During a one-day international at Lahore, he noticed that I was stuttering in my run-up. He told me that rhythm was essential for a fast bowler, that if you get to the crease straining and off balance you have little hope of getting the ball in the right place. Control was vital. Better to cut down my run-up, so that I'd be able to explode at the crease with control over my action. I was running from twenty-five yards to the popping crease at that stage, so I started from seventeen instead. It felt all right, but I knew that I had to perfect it. I couldn't just change run-ups during a hectic international season. It all clicked during my first tour to England in 1987. Just before the first Test at Old Trafford, I was experimenting in the nets with different angles of delivery – going around the wicket, then over the wicket, exploring the areas of the popping crease – just to see what would discomfort a batsman. I decided to sort out my run-up once and for all. Walking two steps, I then sprinted another seventeen paces; it felt comfortable, I was in control, and the ball came out of my hand at the right time. That run-up hasn't altered since. At times it does put a strain on my body as I have a tendency to tear in too quickly and bowl in a rush. I bowl almost in my run-up, with a short delivery stride, and although I'm told that's to my advantage – because there isn't much time to line up my deliveries, it's on to the batsman quickly – it has led to some painful injuries. My groin, hernia and left shoulder have all suffered at various stages, but that's the price you pay for your action. Every fast bowler has injury troubles at some stage. Dennis Lillee had the perfect action, but he had serious back problems and eventually knee injuries, so nobody can escape the ravages to the body.

So, with my technical knowledge expanding, Imran decided I needed some practical experience of bowling in English conditions. He organised a summer for me in league cricket, up in Durham with Burnopfield. Imran felt that, with the Pakistan tour to England a year away, I needed to find out how to bowl on those soft pitches, where seamers were often more dominant than swing bowlers. So the summer of 1986 was spent shivering in the north-east of England, earning fifty pounds a week in the local league. It wasn't an enjoyable experience on a personal level; I was only twenty and I missed my friends and family. Living on my own and without a car, I didn't have much to do, especially when we only played at weekends. It was also a cold, damp summer and I used to get thoroughly miserable whenever a game was rained off. All I wanted to do that summer was play cricket, as often as possible. The standard wasn't all that high – which probably explains why I scored the first hundred of my life and took eight wickets in an innings, including a hat-trick – but at least that period acquainted me with the necessary disciplines for bowling in England. On soft wickets, I realised that I had to go for a fuller length, pitching it about three feet further up than in Pakistan. So the yorker became particularly useful and the bouncer was used sparingly. I found that if I dug the ball in, it would simply sit up slowly and beg to be hooked or pulled away. Imran was right: it was an invaluable learning process for me.

It was clear to me that Imran viewed our forthcoming tour to England in 1987 with the utmost importance. He had been aggrieved when Pakistan lost there in 1982, a close series that could have gone either way. We all knew how keen he was to turn the tables, and the months leading up to that tour were hectic for Pakistan's players. That hasn't changed much over the years, though! We seem to play somwhere in the world almost every month in the year, but at least that gives us the chance to develop our techniques and give our young players vital experience of the big time. That was definitely in my favour as we built towards the trip to England. We had two high-pressure series, the first against West Indies at home which finished one-all, a creditable effort by us against the world's best side. I got the man of the match award at Faisalabad, taking six wickets and slogging my first Test fifty, but more importantly we won the game.

At that stage, I considered myself a bowler who could smash a few runs if lucky, coming in at number nine or ten. My captain saw it differently. In some of the one-day internationals he'd put me in up the order, ahead of established batsmen, with instructions to blaze away. These days that would be called a pinch-hitter, but I saw myself as a slogger. It was fun, but after I made that sixty-six in the Faisalabad Test, Imran said I could be an all-rounder if I puty my mind to it. I kept quiet, nodding as he told me I had the talent for batting. I didn't tell him that no one had ever bothered to coach me in batting, that the spinners usually got me because I'd make up my mind to charge them before they bowled, that concentration at the crease was very difficult for me, and that my eyesight wasn't very good anway. I was just so happy that a great player, and my idol, was prepared to give up so much of his time to encourage me and praise me freely. To a young player, that is a huge boost.

We had an even bigger boost to our confidence before the England tour when we went to India and, for the first time, won the Test series. That victory, after four draws, came in the last Test in Bangalore when our spinners, Iqbal Qasim and Abdul Qadir, brought us home by just sixteen runs. This after we had been bowled out for just 116 in our first innings. It was interesting to see how the pressure of the situation got to the most experienced players like Ravi Shastri and Kapil Dev, who got themselves out rashly when the game was theirs in the final innings. To watch Sunil Gavaskar's ninety-six on a turning pitch was also a great education. He batted for five and half hours, with little trouble, until he was caught at slip off one that took off. That innings by Gavaskar demonstrated the kind of class that bowlers are up against at the highest level. I found myself wondering how I could ever dismiss a player with such beautiful footwork, correct defence, sharp eyesight, and clean strokeplay.

I did manage to make a couple of major contributions in that series. In the first Test, at Madras, Imran and I added 112 for the eighth wicket, a record against India. I enjoyed myself with five sixes in my sixty-two, but the real class came from Imran. He played for me when I was hitting the ball around, then when I got out he upped the tempo. When the last man joined him he was on sixty-eight, but he then scored sixty-seven out of eighty-one for the last wicket, ending unbeaten. It was an object lesson in how to shape a Test match innings. Imran's achievements as an all-rounder gave him a great deal of credibility when he sat down and told his players what he expected of them. Here was one leader who practised what he preached. He had huge charisma and cricketing knowledge; he was a man you followed. He made you perform above yourself by personal example as well as vocal support. When I took five wickets in the next Test in Calcutta, the fact that I did it opening the bowling with Imran was doubly satisfying. I was beginning to get the hang of fast bowling, and his input had so much to do with that.

That tour to India came at a perfect time in my development. Every Pakistani cricket fan has grown up wanting to beat India above all teams. I have always got on very well with the Indian players, but you can't help getting pumped up when you play them, for obvious historical reasons, and the fanatical supporters spur you on as well. On that 1987 tour, our one-day international at Calcutta was played in front of more than 90,000 fans and we were inspired, scraping home by two wickets after chasing six an over throughout innings. Learning to cope with such pressure is essential for an aspiring international cricketer and that tour to India gave me a marvellous grounding.

In my career, many have been kind enough to say that I seem to be able to raise my game for the big occasion, and certainly I love performing to my best in front of a packed house, even if the majority of the spectators are either hostile or supporting the other team. I'm sure those early years in the Pakistan team, getting terrific advice from the senior players and playing so much all over the globe, had a lot to do with my subsequent successes. Temperament is crucial when it comes to performing to your absolute peak on a consistent basis. I was also lucky that the sheer volume of cricket I played for Pakistan before my twenty-first birthday gave me the right training ground to develop my bowling technique. Someone similar to me might have struggled to break through so quickly elsewhere because of the lack of opportunities, but by the time I was twenty-one, all the technical aspects of my bowling were more or less in place: the ability to swing, the surprise element of reverse swing, the run-up, the yorker, when to bowl around the wicket. I knew more or less what I was doing with the ball for the 1987 tour to England onwards.

CHAPTER 4

Falling Out with England

I WENT to England in May 1987 eager and excited, thrilled to be playing for my country where the game of cricket originated. The prospect of playing a Test match at Lord's, the home of cricket, was tremendous, and if we managed to win the series that would be even better. Well we did, and I performed satisfactorily enough, but it was a controversial series with no love lost between the two sides. And things got even worse when we played a return series in Pakistan a few months later, with the England captain having a furious, foul-mouthed row on the field with one of our umpires, followed by the real risk of England walking out on the series and flying home. By the end of the year both sets of players were sick of the sight of each other, and the divisions weren't healed for several more years. Pakistan and England cricketers just didn't get on around that period, and as a result the disagreements stacked up, misunderstandings multiplied, and the press had a field day.

All this was way above my head during that first tour to England. We had already played each other in two short tournaments early in 1987 – the Perth Challenge Cup in Australia, and the Sharjah Trophy. The atmosphere between the two sides could best be described as frosty. Mike Gatting, England's captain against us in Australia, seemed arrogant, looking down his nose at us. His first England tour ten years earlier had been to Pakistan, and after being given out lbw for nought on his Test debut, he seemed to be unhappy about being in our country. Ian Botham was also playing in Australia, and he too was cocky towards us. He came home early from the 1984 tour to Pakistan for a knee operation and gave a radio interview in which he described our country – I quote directly – as 'the kind of place to send your mother-in-law to, all expenses paid'. I thought that was a stupid statement. He didn't seem to understand that people love their own country whatever he might feel, and it's best to keep your mouth shut in such situations. It was highly disrespectful of him and no one in Pakistan has ever forgotten his tactless remarks. When I knew that I'd be bowling at Botham in England, I vowed to bounce him as often as I could. I have always found an extra yard of pace for Ian Botham.

With the likes of Botham and Gatting ignoring us during those games in Australia, the majority of the England players followed suit, and there was no fraternisation after the games were over. Yet I'd see the English guys socialising with the Aussies at the ground and wonder why they were happy to laugh and joke with each other while freezing out the Pakistanis. I asked Imran about this and he replied, 'We don't play county cricket, the English players just don't know us.' I thought about that, but then realised that the Aussies hardly featured in county cricket at that time either. As the months passed that year, it dawned on me that there had been a lot of accumulated grievances on both sides, and a lack of mutual understanding had arisen which would lead to some sad incidents.

From a personal point of view, I loved the tour of England. It was great fun to be with the younger boys in the squad, and travelling around on a coach rather than a plane meant we could see a lot of the countryside, compared with other tours around the world. Imran also drove me around in his sponsored car, making sure I wasn't too distracted by the other boys in the squad. He talked cricket to me on those journeys, telling me I had the talent but, 'You have to work like a dog, Wasim.' Good advice, and I listened closely. He had praised me highly to the press at the start of the tour, saying I would be the world's greatest all-rounder one day. When Imran rated you, he never expressed any doubts about your capabilities, but I wasn't embarrassed about the fact that I was clearly one of his blue-eyed boys. He was very loyal to those he had spotted, as long as they repaid his faith with hard work. That was the main thing I learned from him – that hard work has to back up ability. I never found it an extra pressure to be praised publicly by Imran Khan, I found it inspirational that my hero was telling everyone else that I was meeting his own high standards.

Imran's leadership and ability held Pakistan together to win that series. The first two Tests were badly affected by rain, and he was struggling with a stomach muscle injury during that period. We came to the third Test, at Leeds, with our captain fully fit and he brilliantly exploited the conditions. The bounce was uneven, the wicket had cracks everywhere, and Imran took ten wickets in the match to bowl England out cheaply twice. We won by an innings, and it was a fascinating example of a captain rousing himself after injury for a supreme effort when the chance of victory presented itself. That's something the great players possess – the knack of raising their game when it's really necessary. You need to want it to happen for you. Imran did it again in the next Test at Edgbaston, when we should have lost on the final afternoon as England chased runs. He had hung around a long time in our second innings, frustrating the England bowlers and making sure the rest of the tail followed his lead. He was always very hot on the importance of the last few in the batting order supporting an established player, saying that runs from the lower order meant that team spirit was good. Finally, though, we were all out and England needed 124 from eighteen overs for a win that would square the series. In a Test match, that was a tall order, but England were bound to look at it as a one-day target and go for it.

Before we took the field, our captain said to us: 'Make sure they don't get them, be brave, try your best.' He led from the front, opening the bowling with me, and although England got a brisk start, we rallied and saved the game. They finished fifteen short as we bowled throughout with pace and accuracy. They started to panic and lost seven wickets, getting very frustrated. It was a great feeling for us to save that Test, which allowed us to go to the last one at the Oval safe from defeat in the series. For me it was a double pleasure because I got Ian Botham out twice at Edgbaston. I caught and bowled him, then in the second innings, after he had been promoted up the order, I did him for pace with a quick bouncer and had him caught off a top-edged hook. I also hit him for six over mid-wicket in that match and he swore at me, which made me laugh in his face. After getting him caught at slip at Lord's off a quick bouncer, then hitting him on the toe at Leeds with a yorker that meant he couldn't bowl at all in the match, I reckon I won the battle with him that series. It gave me particular pleasure after his hostile attitude to us and to our country.

We had much the better of a high-scoring draw at the Oval, with Botham and Gatting having to bat out the last five hours to save the game. So we won the series, but I couldn't celebrate with the boys: I was in hospital having an appendix operation after being taken ill on the fourth evening. But I was soon well enough to appreciate the extent of our achievement. England had started the series on a high, having beaten Australia comfortably a few months earlier, and they gave the impression that they expected to beat us. That fired us up, especially as they made no attempt to be friendly at close of play or in the morning before the start. Only Neil Foster, Phil Edmonds and David Gower showed any friendship towards us on and off the field; no one else spoke a word. It was almost as if they were trying to freeze us out. Compare that attitude to the Indian series earlier in the year, whether the rivalry was so much more intense yet both sets of players got along well enough when the day's play was over.

It was clear to us that most of the England players thought we were moaners and cheats, and there was one regrettable incident involving one of our players that reflected badly on us. At Leeds Botham was incensed by an appeal for a catch by our wicketkeeper, Salim Yousuf. Many felt he had already dropped the ball, caught it on the rebound, and still appealed – it was really embarrassing. Imran promptly gave Salim an angry dressing-down in front of everyone, and in full view of the television cameras, leaving no one in doubt that he took a dim view, but Botham didn't help matters by his fevered reaction: he squared up to Salim and using foul language threatened to punch him. It added to the feeling among English players that the Pakistanis would stop at nothing, but I do believe that this stupid appeal by Salim was an exception.

Perhaps Botham's anger at Salim had been simmering before the incident. Before Botham came in, Salim had won an appeal for a catch behind off Imran to dismiss Chris Broad. The TV replay showed that Broad had been unlucky because he had taken his hand away from the bat handle when the ball brushed his glove, which is not out. But Broad's former county colleague David Shepherd had given the decision, so he couldn't complain about biased umpiring. It all happened so quickly, with the ball lifting away sharply off the pitch, that the bowler and wicketkeeper were bound to appeal. Botham and all the other England bowlers had done the same in the past and would do so again, so they couldn't really gripe at the rub of the green this time. It was one of those things, a mistake by a good umpire uncovered by TV replays, but the English players seemed to think it was all our fault. A few months later, Chris Broad was to show his contempt for our umpires in the Lahore Test when he refused to walk after being given out. No doubt that unlucky dismissal at Leeds preyed on his mind and contributed to his making a fool of himself.

This question of umpiring was at the root of England's dislike of Pakistan around this period. They felt we had no justification for complaints about the quality of umpiring in England when ours was so poor back home. The argument was: 'They cheat us back at their place, now they've got the cheek to whinge about ours when they make an occasional mistake.' Lots of horror stories had circulated over the years about the useless Pakistani umpires, that visiting sides had to get fifteen wickets instead of ten to bowl us out, that Javed Miandad was never given out lbw during Tests at home. Botham and Gatting had toured in Pakistan and they weren't slow to castigate our umpires, as well as our country. So the atmosphere was soured right from the start of that 1987 series in England, especially when Imran Khan continued to press publicly for neutral umpires. He had felt for several years that relationships between sides would improve if the standing umpires were selected from two test-playing countries other than those contesting the series. He accepted there were umpiring faults all over the world, but that at least the suspicion of home bias would be eradicated if umpires were from a third country.

All this was new to me on my first tour of England, and I asked my captain why he kept hammering home this point year after year. He said it stemmed from the Leeds Test of 1982, when he believed we were cheated out of victory by poor umpiring. He was particularly scathing about David Constant, and was angry that he was due to stand in the 1987 series despite an official protest from our management. Imran didn't like Constant's manner, which he considered rude and abrupt, quite apart from his perceived defects as an umpire. He was also dismayed to see Kim Palmer on the panel, because the captain felt he was also inadequate in 1982. On top of that, Imran told me that the Indians had objected to Constant when they toured England in 1982 and their wish had been granted, with Constant standing down for that series. So why couldn't that precedent be followed up on our behalf five years later? He felt that the request had been put politely at the start of our 1987 tour, without informing the press, but the Test and County Cricket Board had dug its heels in and made it clear English cricket wouldn't be pushed around by the Pakistanis. During the Lord's Test, the TCCB's chief executive, A. C. Smith, read out a statement to the press from the first-class umpires which supported their colleagues on that year's umpiring Test panel. So it was now out in the open, and the battle lines were being drawn up.

Our tour manager, Haseeb Ahsan, was always happy to talk about our grievances to the press and I'm sure that some of his more excitable comments didn't help our cause or image. He described Constant as 'a disgraceful person', and condemned the quality of his umpiring, observations unlikely to calm things down or make the England players view us in a more favourable light. We couldn't shake off the reputation of whingers who were conditioned to sharp practice, while we took the attitude of setting out to beat their umpires as well as their players. It rankled with Imran and some of the senior players that Pakistan hadn't been given a full tour of England since 1962, when we were still weak. Now he felt that we were a big draw, especially with such a large Pakistani community in England, and so we deserved wider prominence. I'm sure there was also the underlying feeling that it was fun to beat the country that had ruled us before Partition forty years earlier. All that was too much for a youngster to grasp in 1987 – all I wanted to do was enjoy my cricket and see the team win – but such issues enhanced the deep pleasure Imran felt on winning the series. He is a very proud Pakistani, and to beat India and England away from home in the space of six months was one of his career highlights.

As for me, I felt I was a better player for the experience of that England tour. I didn't think I bowled consistently well, struggling with my length on the slow, damp pitches, but I ended up with more first-class wickets on the tour than anyone else. Javed and Imran used to tell me on that tour, 'The more you play, the better you become,' and it was hard to argue with that. I had crammed so much into a first-class career that was not yet three years old. There were other young players coming through from that trip who would serve Pakistan proud: Salim Malik, Ramiz Raja, and Ijaz Ahmed. It was a tremendously exciting time to be starting a Test career.

And the excitement kept on coming for me. Next on the agenda – the 1987 World Cup. Getting the chance to play in that at the age of twenty-one was a privilege, even if we failed to make it to the final. We were the tournament favourites, which made sense as it was held in India and Pakistan, and we topped our qualifying group with five wins out of six. Imran and Abdul Qadir had bowled superbly in those early games, but we couldn't raise ourselves in the semi-final against Australia at Lahore. We made a bad start, chasing 268 in fifty overs; I failed at number six, looking to accelerate, and although Imran and Javed did their best we just couldn't dominate some excellent Australian bowling and fielding. They won by eighteen runs, and for the third successive World Cup Pakistan had lost in the semi-finals. This was a blow, especially losing in front of my home crowd in Lahore.

We had beaten England twice in the World Cup games – by eighteen runs in Rawalpindi and seven wickets in Karachi – and that clearly displeased them. So when the England tour of Pakistan started just a week after they had narrowly lost the final to Australia, the omens for a harmonious series weren't exactly favourable. This would be our fifth tournament involving England in 1987, and there had been no time for simmering down. They would expect poor umpiring, and after the comments of Imran and Haseeb Ahsan a few months earlier, England would no doubt retaliate in public if they had a grievance. Imran's absence from this series was another worry. He announced his retirement after the World Cup tournament, although he was eventually persuaded to return to the fold a few months later. He usually managed to keep a lid on some of the more volatile players in our side, but with Javed Miandad replacing him as captain, there would be increased tension. Javed, a fighter on an off the field, thrived on controversy. He used to abuse the bowlers when he was batting just to get himself fully motivated. Javed would seek out grievances, and he certainly didn't care for the England players he had faced over the previous decade. So the chemistry wasn't right at the start of the series, particularly between the two captains, Javed and Gatting. Both of them must take a great deal of responsibility for the disgraceful scenes that happened, with Gatting the major culprit in my opinon.

Even I, still a novice, knew that Pakistani umpires weren't good enough at the start of that volatile series. I don't believe they were cheats, though, who favoured us unduly. You have to remember that our umpires at that time didn't get a great deal of practical experience standing in Tests. Imran used to say to them at the start of a home series: 'Now I want you to be fair and firm on the field, make your decisions in a confident manner, and don't be intimidated by either side.' He never put them under pressure. Javed was a different case. He didn't have Imran's leadership skills, calming the boys down and telling them off for making ridiculous appeals.

The first flashpoint came in the Lahore Test when Chris Broad refused to leave the crease after being given out, caught behind. Now I am the first to agree that the umpiring in the first Test was disgraceful, that it favoured us. Mike Gatting was given out lbw, sweeping Abdul Qadir when the ball had pitched on leg stump and was going down legside. He had a justifiable grievance over that decision, but his mood quickly spread to the rest of his side, especially to Broad. It was astonishing and embarrassing to see Broad stand his ground, wagging a gloved finger, saying he hadn't touched the ball and wasn't going. His partner, Graham Gooch, had to come down to his end and persuade him to go. It seemed to take ages before he dragged himself from the crease, with swearwords flying around between batsman and close fielders. To this day I don't know what Broad was thinking about, because he *was* out. I was standing nearby, at short mid-wicket, and there was a definite noise. It was a good decision, admittedly a rarity in that match. I had to turn my back during Broad's performance, I was so stunned that he felt he wasn't out.

Mind you, we had got used to Broad's reactions to his dismissals at our hands. I remembered the controversial decision at Leeds a few months earlier when he was unlucky, but I hadn't forgotten the fuss he made when I had him caught behind for nought at Perth in January. The television replay showed the ball brushed his hip and didn't make contact with his gloves or bat, but to the naked eye it didn't appear that way. I heard a noise, there was a hurried movement from the batsman, and I did what any bowler does in such situations – appeal for a catch by the keeper. He was given out and stomped off in a rage, the same reaction he showed in the previous one-day game at Perth when Imran had him caught behind for ninety-seven. Each time we appealed in good faith and he was given out by Australian umpires. Judging by Chris Broad's attitude in 1987, he would be the best one to judge whether he was in or out, not the umpire. If the umpire happened to be a Pakistani, that was even more cut and dried – not out. He was typical of England's arrogance on that tour of Pakistan.

It was astonishing that Broad wasn't sent home after his dreadful petulance in Lahore. Instead he was given a mild rebuke and wasn't even fined. So the scene was set for the deplorable incident between Gatting and umpire Shakoor Rana in the next Test at Faisalabad. Now I must underline that I have some sympathy with England over some of their complaints. Gatting was perfectly entitled to file a complaint about the standard of umpiring in Lahore, and it was wrong that he didn't find out who would be umpiring in the next Test until the press told him. That was disrespectful. As we had demonstrated on our recent tour to England, the visiting side is within its rights to protest at the appointment of a designated umpire, as long as it is handled in the proper manner and through the necessary channels. Our board of control didn't behave with dignity or proper respect towards England, and I'm sure that if Imran had been captain things would have been handled differently. It suited Javed Miandad to have England furious at the umpiring, complaining about being ignored at official levels, because all that would reduce their effectiveness as a team. We were already one-nil up in the series with two to play, so Javed was going to give them nothing.

A groin injury kept me out of the Faisalabad Test, but I watched it at home on television and I couldn't believe what I was missing when Gatting and Shakoor Rana flew at each other, cursing face to face. It looked awful, terrible, and the pictures all over the papers next day shamed the game of cricket. So many factors were involved, not least England's growing frustration. I had some sympathy with Gatting on that point because he was behind in the Test series, suffering from a strong sense of grievance, feeling that he was having to combat two umpires as well as eleven players. Yet what he was doing on the field when Shakoor Rana intervened was wrong. He was moving a fielder behind the batsman's back when the bowler was running in. That can easily be construed as cheating, or at least trying to take advantage. Now I know Gatting didn't mean to take any advantage, but why did he fly off the handle at the umpire? The umpire's intervention wasn't all that important; it didn't concern a decision about a possible dismissal, it was just about the ethics of moving a fielder at the wrong time. Gatting ought to have apologised straight away and got on with the game, and that would have been the end of it. Instead he allowed himself to get dragged into a dreadful row.

Now I knew Shakoor Rana well. I used to play cricket on the streets with his sons, and he is an excitable character, very loud, not averse to a swear-word when necessary. He was always very hot on players' discipline on the field. I've seem him bark at a bowler if he appealed too much and tell him loudly to get back to his mark. He lacked diplomacy, but for a long time I thought he was one of Pakistan's best umpires – admittedly not a very high recommendation. Yet he was right to stop the game and reprimand Gatting, even though he could have done so with more diplomacy. The umpire has to be respected on the field of play and the rules say he is the sole judge of how the game should be played out there. If only Gatting had taken a deep breath and ignored his understandable frustrations, it would have been cleared up. Once he had dug his heels in and Javed Miandad got involved, the dispute was bound to escalate. Javed reminded Shakoor Rana about the slur on his country, and the umpire then demanded an apology from Gatting. I could see how Shakoor had now been boxed into a corner by Javed; umpires didn't earn a great deal of money in Pakistan in 1987, and he wasn't likely to go against the advice of Pakistan's captain. So we then had the farce of umpire waiting for England captain's written apology, a day's play completely abandoned during all the deliberations, and England leaving with a draw when they might just have won, with a bit of luck. And self-control.

If there was any sympathy at all for Gatting and his players, it disappeared immediately when officials from the TCCB flew out to persuade them to carry on with the tour. We were amazed to hear that all the English players had been given a hardship bonus of £1,000. This was astonishing, and the term 'hardship bonus' suggested to the outside world that it was a terrible strain being on a cricket tour to Pakistan. They should have been with us in Sri Lanka the previous year when the umpiring was far worse than in this series and crowd disturbances very serious, with Javed Miandad being hit by a rock as he walked back to the pavilion. You didn't hear the Pakistanis looking for a hardship bonus then, even though we were very worried about the volatile atmosphere on that tour. We felt that England's players were just being cry-babies, with their management telling them to keep their heads down and take the extra money, the implication being that they had been badly treated in Pakistan and were justified in their public moaning.

It's true that some of the umpiring decisions were poor, but does that explain why Abdul Qadir took thirty wickets in three Tests? The truth is that they couldn't play a top leg spinner bang in form and they just looked for excuses. After the first Test in Lahore, England's tour manager Peter Lush told the press that nine bad decisions went the way of Pakistan's bowlers. What qualifications did he have to make that comment, other than just churning out the propaganda from the England dressing-room? To the best of my knowledge, Mr Lush had not played cricket for England, so if he was giving his personal assessment of those decisions he had no practical knowledge or experience to call on. He was just as rash as Haseeb Ahsan had been with some of his inflammatory statements on the England tour, but Mr Lush was on more secure ground when he called for neutral umpires after the Lahore Test. At last! England was starting to see the logic of Pakistan's proposal that they had rejected for years!

It was ridiculous for England to get £1,000 extra per man for seeing through the tour when they ought to have been proud to represent their country. Apart from the more isolated and smaller venues on that tour, they were staying in five-star hotels, as good as anywhere on the international circuit. You pick up the phone and everything is sorted out for you in those hotels. The English public ought to know that in Pakistan we are hospitable, and there was no difference on that particular tour. Visiting cricketers are treated like VIPs in our country. There's no hanging around at customs or passport control, they are garlanded with flowers as soon as they arrive, and whisked straight to their hotels without delay, with their luggage brought to their rooms later. Compare our two tours to England, in 1987 and 1992. On each occasion it took us six hours to get out of Heathrow airport after we had been comprehensively searched for drugs. We had sniffer dogs around us all the time and every bag, pair of boots, batting gloves, and bat was minutely examined to see if anyone was smuggling in illegal substances. It was not a pleasant experience after such a long, tiring flight from Pakistan and didn't exactly make us feel we were welcome in the United Kingdom. In Pakistan the atmosphere is totally different, the welcome is warm and genuine. One day I'd love to see English and Australian cricketers have to stand in various queues at the airport when they arrive, then hang around to pick up their own buggage. But it doesn't happen; their players are spoiled because we treat them like honoured guests. Hardly a justification for a hardship bonus!

When I returned for the final Test in Karachi, the atmosphere between the two sides was hostile, the worst I had experienced so far in my short career. No one was talking to each other and it was so unreal. I kept thinking 'What's going on? Is this the way to play cricket? Can it get any worse? I hadn't banked on anything like this, and to my naive eyes it all seemed so unnecessary. If we had been able to use neutral umpires, I'm certain some of the excesses would have been avoided. It takes two to make a quarrel, and there's no doubt that we had contributed our share towards the breakdown in the relationship. All the baggage and the gossip from previous encounters had been brought to this series and there was a lack of open-mindedness in both camps. The main blame in my eyes has to be laid at the door of the England captain and management for allowing the situation to fester throughout 1987, and for losing self-control at Lahore and Faisalabad. They will say they could take no more, that they were being cheated out of Test matches, but did they seriously believe they were the only ones to suffer on international tours? Every touring side comes back with hard-luck stories of varying degrees, and Pakistan have been at fault themselves. Some of our behaviour on the field in my time has been inexcusable, and the management weak. It all comes down to strong captaincy, and Gatting was too ready to act the martyr on this 1987 tour. It's not as if he was new to playing in Pakistan, with all the frustrations – he'd been there twice with England before he blew his top in 1987.

Perhaps it was worse for England to lose against Pakistan than any other country. Certainly the chemistry was volatile between us during that period, and it didn't exactly improve in the next few years. Those unhappy, sour experiences were uppermost in my mind when I captained the Pakistan tour party to England for the first time, in 1996. I was very pleased that we seemed to have built a few important bridges after that series, because I was only too painfully aware of the bad blood that passed between us during my early days in the Pakistan side. Playing in a happy, supportive Lancashire side had certainly helped me understand English cricketers better. That move to Old Trafford was to be one of the best decisions I ever made.

CHAPTER 5

Taking Extra Responsibility

S IGNING FOR Lancashire in 1988 was absolutely crucial in my development as a cricketer. It gave me responsibility as an overseas player in the county championship, the awareness that I was expected to be a matchwinner at various stages through-out an English summer that involved four competitions. Joining a high-profile club like Lancashire was a lucrative deal for me at the age of twenty-one, but I knew I had to perform for them. Imran wouldn't be there to guide me, sing my praises to the media, and get my head round the bad days. I was on my own at last as a cricketer, after an apprenticeship that had lasted just over three years.

The English experience undoubtedly helped me as a cricketer and continued a development that peaked in 1992, the year Pakistan won the World Cup and were confirmed as one of the best teams in Test cricket. Both times the side that was beaten by us was England. I suppose that's ammunition for those who maintain that it's wrong for overseas players to gain valuable experience in county cricket, only to return to help their country thrash England, but I do believe that, overall, I've given good value to Lancashire.

My first inkling that I might be playing in county cricket came during the Sharjah tournament in April 1987. England were one of our opponents and one of their batsmen, Neil Fairbrother, asked if I would be interested in playing at Lancashire. I said, 'You mean in the Lancashire leagues,' and I was flabbergasted when he said, 'No, for Lancashire in county cricket.' I was honoured that they were thinking of me and a few weeks later I met with their officials in London to negotiate. My tour manager, Haseeb Ahsan, handled the details on my behalf and I was thrilled to sign, ready to play for them the following year. Back home, if you played for an English county you were regarded as a special cricketer. It was seen as a finishing school for a Pakistani player; all those different wickets up and down the country were seen as a major test of your ability to adapt. If you could manage that successfully, the general belief was that you would automatically emerge a better player. That was the driving force behind my acceptance of Lancashire's offer. They were also nice people at Old Trafford, very warm towards me. My twenty-first birthday coincided with the Old Trafford Test of 1987 – my debut against England – and to mark the occasion Lancashire flew my family over from Lahore as a surprise present to me. I was very touched by that. I'm the sort of person who responds to loyalty and kindness, and that gesture will never be forgotten by me. Quite apart from all the other incentives, that human touch really made me want to give of my best to Lancashire. I couldn't wait to get started. It's been a love affair throughout as far as I'm concerned.

There's only been one blot on my copybook on the field, when Lancashire fined me £1,000 for losing my temper in 1991 against Warwickshire, and when I cooled down I realised they were right. I was getting frustrated that I couldn't wrap up the Warwickshire innings, with Dermot Reeve getting under my skin – something he managed with a lot of other players – and Tim Munton just playing forward to block me. So I tried a few bouncers, but got nowhere. I started swearing loudly, and the umpire, Nigel Plews, thought I was cursing him because he had warned me for overuse of the bouncer. I think Plews is a nice guy and a good umpire, and I was actually cursing myself in frustration. After my third warning he ordered me out of the attack, as he is entitled to do. He was right to do so, although I didn't think so at the time. The club didn't want me to get banned, so they slapped the maximum fine on me, because it was seen as a serious offence.

At the time I had one or two indirect offers from other counties, because they saw the headline and assumed I was unhappy, but there was never any prospect of my leaving Lancashire. I've had so much fun with my team-mates, and the administrative staff have been marvellous as well. As for the supporters, well, I think they've enjoyed me. I can fully understand how Lancashire supporters must have felt when I hardly played in the 1997 season. The shoulder injury that had bothered me for at least a year flared up at the wrong time, and at times I was in great pain. Having missed the whole of the 1996 season because I was on the Pakistan tour, the prospect of getting back to Old Trafford and winning more trophies was very exciting to me. It turned out to be the most frustrating time of my career, because I simply couldn't do anything to speed up my recuperation. I know that the Lancashire members have a reputation of speaking their minds, and I was gratified that no one gave me a mouthful during that awful summer. Hopefully everyone realised how much I wanted to be out on the field, trying to do my best for a club that has been so good to me.

It was important to me to make a good, early impression when I arrived at Old Trafford. I'd had a groin operation after the tour to West Indies a few months earlier, but I was fully fit and raring to go when I was met at Heathrow airport by the coach, Alan Ormrod. Next day, I was playing at Trent Bridge against Nottinghamshire. The boys made me very welcome, although it was a shock to be told I had to wear a blazer and tie on the way to a match. I'd been used to tracksuits with Pakistan – this was the real thing! It was a tremendously supportive dressing-room under the wise captaincy of David Hughes, with the younger players encouraged to chip in with their thoughts. That was a change from the Pakistan dressing-room, where you were expected to sit in the corner and listen patiently to the seniors. I remember how cold it was, and the long johns came in very handy, but when I saw the rest of the lads walking around in shorts I thought I'd better do the same! After a while, it didn't feel so cold.

Very quickly, I became a victim of the Lancashire humour. After my first game, I packed away all my gear into my large case – we call them coffins – and carried it out of the Trent Bridge dressing-room, straining and sweating with the effort. I thought: 'Have I suddenly lost all my strength? This coffin's too heavy for me, I'll have to do some weight training.' It was only when I got to Old Trafford that I realised I'd been done. I unpacked all my gear from the coffin and found a large stone at the bottom! No wonder it had felt heavy. I had a good laugh about it in front of the lads, and I was quite pleased, because I felt that a practical joke at my expense was their way of saying they'd accepted me. It wasn't the last time a newcomer to the Old Trafford dressing-room suffered the coffin trick!

For the first few weeks I was a little homesick, despite the warmth of everyone at Old Trafford. There's only so much your team-mates can do for you – and they always included me in any social activities – and it's up to the overseas players to get on with it all and adapt himself as quickly as possible to a new culture. For the first six weeks I lived in a hotel next to the ground, then I bought the house where I've lived ever since, about twenty minutes' drive from Old Trafford. This period was good for me, as I had to find the launderette and shops, doing the sort of domestic things my mother had always done for me. A good friend of mine, Aslam Parvez, who lived in London, would come up and spend time with me, and I called my family regularly. Their advice was always the same: relax and get used to your new life as soon as possible. My mother and gran were no longer there to spoil me and there was no Imran Khan standing at mid-off, telling me what to bowl next. Socially, I knocked around with two of my team-mates, the Sri Lankan Gehan Mendis and the West Indian Patrick Patterson, and in no time I felt at home in the Manchester area.

I was bowled over by the facilities at Old Trafford. Compared to Pakistan, Lancashire's cricketers were so lucky. We had two dressing-room attendants, a large area for yourself, a huge tub, your own towels – all you had to do was put your kit on and go out on the field. I'd feel the smooth, lush outfield under my feet, enjoy the excellent net facilities and the quality of the umpiring, and tell myself I'd finally arrived in the big time. In Pakistan, you had to share one towel and hope the showers were working that day. I tried to tell my new team-mates how spoiled they were, but I don't think they believed me.

I never encountered any hostility from the Lancashire boys, even though relations were strained between out two national sides at that time. They knew I didn't have a hothead reputation, and as soon as they realised how much I cared about winning games for Lancashire, I was readily accepted.

It was all such an adventure; I wanted to play every day. All the travelling didn't bother me because I loved seeing different parts of the English countryside. I managed to get on the right side of the Old Trafford crowd right away by scoring a hundred in my first game there. As it was also my maiden century in first-class cricket, I was pleased with my timing. It was against Somerset, and I can still see the shot that brought up my hundred, a wild slog through mid-wicket off Vic Marks. I had been very nervous when I got to the eighties – unfamiliar territory for me – and I started to hit and hope. I'd come in at number eight, after saying that I batted at number nine back home, carefully concealing the fact that only a year earlier I had been the number eleven in the side. So I got in ahead of good batsmen like Warren Hegg and Jack Simmons, and the later batsmen hung around for me. I was thrilled at the reception I got from the crowd, and it remains one of my happiest memories in cricket. Unfortunately we lost the match, due to the brilliance of Martin Crowe. I bowled fast and managed some reverse swing, but Crowe was outstanding, making over two hundred runs in the game. The boys were downhearted about losing, but I had some consolations. I had proved I could score runs in championship cricket and the fact that the fixtures kept coming on top of one another meant we could get out there and make amends within a day or so. At the time, I didn't appreciate the workload that came with county cricket.

My best game that season was at Southport against Surrey when I did the hat-trick and got us to within one run of victory, scoring ninety-eight in quick time. It was the first time I had performed the hat-trick in first-class cricket, and all three wickets came from around the wicket coming in to the right-hander, hitting middle and off stumps. Ian Greig and Keith Medlycott were the first two victims, and then I had a chat with Gehan Mendis and David Hughes. I was getting some reverse swing and they suggested I go for the yorker. I tore in at the batsman, Mark Feltham, the ball pitched off and middle, swung in late, and it yorked him. It was a marvellous moment as the boys jumped all over me. I was delighted at how pleased they all were for me, because I'd been trying really hard since I'd arrived; I was desperate to make a large impact in every game for Lancashire. This Surrey match was a good one for me statistically – eight wickets and 156 runs – but again we didn't win. We were set 272 off seventy overs, and when I came in we were 129 for 5. I had a go, hit a few sixes, and with three balls left we needed just one to win with two wickets left – and I was on strike. Ian Greig was the bowler and he'd been frustrating me with wide deliveries down the legside. I slogged him for what would be the winning runs and my century, but David Ward at deep mid-wicket ran and ran and took a fine catch. That left Jack Simmons to get one off the last two deliveries, but they were bowled down the legside and Simmo couldn't get near them. Nowadays the umpires would be more strict, calling wides and handing the victory to us, but Grieg got away with it. Annoying. There's little consolation for me in doing well individually if your team doesn't win the game. You want to do your best, but in my opinion the team's fortunes take precedence.

After that Southport match my groin problem flared up again and I missed the last seven championship matches. It also ruled me out of the Test series at home against Australia, and it was a worrying period for me. But at least I could reflect on a good start with Lancashire. I had shown I was capable of performing at county level with both bat and ball. Perhaps Imran was right: I might make an all-rounder one day. My Lancashire team-mates were very generous to me whenever I had success. I wasn't a particularly big name at the time in world cricket, and they saw me as one for the future. In a sense, they felt they'd helped me establish myself on a bigger stage by giving me the chance to play so often against world-class cricketers. I learned such a lot in that 1988 season about the need to pace myself during busy periods, the value of getting a lot of rest, how to prepare mentally then switch on when I took the field. I continued to experiment in the nets, getting accustomed to bowling around the wicket which gave me a different angle for my swing bowling. We talked a lot about cricket, the players we rated, and the best ways to nullify them. I loved the dry English sense of humour, and felt really at home within a few weeks at Old Trafford. My English improved and I learned to speak my mind. Before I was shy and quiet in conversation, only speaking when asked to do so, but I blossomed in England and took part in lively cricket discussions whenever anyone wanted to thrash out something. After just one season with Lancashire, I was definitely a better player and a more mature person. I was on a long contract there and I knew it would always be a pleasure to get back to Old Trafford for a new season – despite the cold!

By the time I reported for county duty again I was in no danger of complaining about being overlooked by the relentless schedule of international cricket. I had hardly played during the intervening months due to that niggling groin injury. I managed a short one-day series in Australia after resting during the West Indies visit to Pakistan, but then broke down in our first game of the New Zealand tour. Initially it was diagnosed as a pelvic fracture, but it turned out to be that recurring groin problem and I simply had to rest. It would be another year before the injury was sorted out with a major operation, and the next few months were uncertain ones for me. I only managed eleven championship matches in the 1989 season, alternating with the other overseas fast bowler, Patrick Patterson. We didn't see each other as rivals – we were good friends and I rated him highly as a fast bowler. He wasn't naturally quick like a Michael Holding or an Allan Donald, but when he got into his rhythm he was devastating. When we both played against the Australians that year, he produced the fastest spell of bowling I've ever seen. He fired out Mike Veletta and David Boon in his first over and really made the other batsmen hop around on that first evening. It was fun to watch, but not to face, and I declined the request to field in the slips to Patto. I said I was very happy standing at mid-on!

Lancashire had their best season that year since 1971, and we won the Sunday League after a gap of nineteen years. That was a fantastic day. We beat Surrey by seven wickets with Paul Allott hitting a six to win it in the final over, and soon we were drenched in champagne. Our home crowd showered us with drinks and it was wonderful to share the winning moment with the guys who had become my great friends. I had broken Lancashire's Sunday League record of wickets as well, so it was a double celebration for me. It would have been great to win the championship as well after being one of the front-runners for much of the summer, but we ran out of steam and the two overseas players were unfit at bad times, with five championship matches played that didn't feature either myself or Patto. Frustration at failing to land the title was to prove a recurring theme throughout my time at Old Trafford, despite our great success in one-day matches.

Although I'd like to have played more championship matches, I was happy with a return of fifty wickets in those eleven games, finishing just behind Allan Donald and Malcolm Marshall at the top of the first-class averages. My happiest memory was the ten wickets I took in the Roses match at Old Trafford, when we easily beat our great rivals Yorkshire. I believe that was the first time the English cricket public saw what reverse swing was all about. The match was televised live in the north of England and I understand that Fred Trueman, one of the TV summarisers, was amazed at the amount of late swing I was getting. It was no great secret as far as I was concerned. In the nets I'd worked hard at perfecting late swing from around the wicket, making my body turn more into a sideways position so that I could get the ball to move in the air. I'd told my Lancashire team-mates about the ideal conditions to get the ball to reverse – dry, hot, with the ball roughed up one side after about forty overs' use – and yet I was the only one using that technique at the time in English cricket. To me it was just a case of being curious, trying new methods to make the ball swing, to get batsmen playing down the wrong line, looking for outswing when the ball suddenly darts inwards at a good pace.

I was surprised that my colleagues didn't try to experiment with reverse swing when it was obviously working for me, but during that period they kept talking about line and length, about bowling in 'the corridor of uncertainty' on or around the off-stump. That was all very well against average players on wickets that helped the bowler, but when you come up against top batsmen on flat wickets they'll just whip such deliveries through mid-wicket all day, or, if they're not feeling in the mood, let the delivery go by harmlessly. Six of my ten victims were clean bowled in that Lancashire match, and it was simply a case of utilising ideal weather for reverse swing. A few more years were to pass before English bowlers began to see the value of this technique.

That hard work in the nets had set me up for the next big step in my international career. After two seasons with Lancashire I was confident I'd mastered the basics of swing bowling, building on the knowledge passed on to me by Imran Khan. The next few months in international cricket justified my renewed confidence. We won the Sharjah Trophy, winning all four matches against India and the West Indies, and I got a hat-trick to beat the West Indies when it looked as if we were certain to lose. Needing 251, they were 209 for 5 at one stage, but I took four wickets in thirteen balls. From around the wicket I hit the leg stumps of Jeffrey Dujon and Malcolm Marshall and then asked Imran's advice for the next delivery, to Curtly Ambrose. 'Go over the wicket,' he said. 'Bowl him an outswinger, because he'll be expecting the inswinger. Keep your head still.' It pitched middle and hit off-stump, the ideal ball for a hat-trick. Just to round off a perfect spell, I bowled Courtney Walsh going around the wicket, hitting middle and off. It was a marvellous occasion, a packed crowd of 25,000 roaring us on against a strong West Indies side including Viv Richards, Desmond Haynes and Richie Richardson, and it was screened live on TV in Pakistan. It was even more exciting in the next match, against India. With passions running high in the crowd, divided in their volatile support, our target was 274 in forty-six overs. Imran sent me in at number three with instructions to get after the bowling, and I loved it. I blocked the first ball, just to get a sighter, but the next one went over mid-wicket for six. I hit four sixes in my thirty-seven off twenty-two balls and helped to set up a successful run chase.

I managed another crucial six a week or so later to help us win the Nehru Cup in front of more than 70,000 spectators in Calcutta. This one-day tournament, held in India, featured all the Test countries apart from New Zealand, and we got through to the final by beating England. The West Indies had looked in ominous form and a target of 274 in fifty overs was steep against bowlers of the calibre of Ambrose, Marshall and Walsh. Viv Richards gambled by bowling out his quicks, so he had to bowl the final over. I walked in to bat in that last over with the crowd baying for a West Indian victory – don't forget, this was in India. Imran Khan was waiting for me with, as usual, some stern advice: 'Just block it, play back and take a single,' he commanded. 'Give me the strike.' It was had to argue with his logic, because he had played superbly for his fifty-five not out and we needed three to win off the last two balls.

It made sense to give him the final delivery of the match. So I was determined to play for my captain when Richards sent me down a good-length ball, coming into my legs. Then I disobeyed instructions, hitting it over mid-wicket for six. As we ran off the field, Irman shouted, 'I told you to block it!' and after shouting, 'It was in the slot!' I just kept on running.

It just got better and better for me during that typically hectic period of Pakistan cricket. Next on the agenda was a home Test series against India, an encounter we all eagerly anticipated. All four Tests were drawn, with large totals being made by both sides, and I was very pleased to end up with eighteen wickets in the series, the highest total on either side. I bowled more overs than anyone else and felt full of fire, loving that special rivarly between our two countries. The atmosphere between the two sides in that series was very good for one particular reason: neutral umpires. At last Imran had got his way. John Holder and John Hampshire came over from England and impressed everyone with their calmness and fairness. Of course they made mistakes, as all human beings do, but their decisions were accepted without any fuss because no one could accuse them of bias. It seemed such an obvious way to improve relations between international cricketers when the pressure to win was increasing all the time, yet it was to be another four years before the ICC sanctioned the use of neutral umpires. Even then the rule didn't go all the way, because only one neutral umpire per Test was to be allowed.

My confidence was very high by the time we got to Australia for a one-day series and three Tests, and it turned out to be my most productive tour so far. In the Test series I averaged almost forty with the bat, took seventeen wickets, and although we lost one-nil we competed hard with Australia. They were on a roll after beating England four-nil, and our efforts meant we could fairly claim to be in the world's top three. I was particularly pleased with my batting, scoring my first Test hundred, and it seemed I was at last grasping the truth that not every ball has to be hit out of the ground. Before the Test series started I had managed to play sensibly in one of the one-day finals, at Melbourne. When I came in we were 50 for 5 with Carl Rackemann and Terry Alderman right on top, enjoying a rain-affected wicket. For a long time I just blocked everything, determined not to get out. My mental game was very strong that night, and I ended up with eighty-six out of 110 added when I was at the crease. We lost the game easily enough after making only 162, but I was happy with the way I built my innings.

I picked up eleven wickets in the first Test at Melbourne, but I was disappointed with the standard of umpiring. They got six lbw verdicts in our second innings when we were hanging on for the draw, and at least three of them were missing leg stump. We could easily have come away with an honourable draw, and that would have been a fine effort after being bowled out for 107 on a quick pitch, with cracks appearing regularly. It was an ideal surface for me to bowl orthodox seam at a good pace and I enjoyed it, but we were so close to saving the game.

We managed to do that in the next Test at Adelaide, though. My first Test hundred came at the crucial moment for my side. In the second innings we were 90 for 5 when I joined Imran, and with Australia having built a handy lead, we were in effect 6 for 5. Although we were in deep trouble, with Merv Hughes roaring in and being very free with his verbals, I felt in good nick, having hit a rapid fifty in the first innings, and Imran said: 'Play your normal game, just like you did the other day, but pick your shots, don't slog.' We stayed together for four hours, adding 191, and when I outscored Imran I was quietly content. He set such high standards for himself that you felt you had to try extra hard to measure up to him and earn his approval. He could be very stern if he felt let down by one of his favourites, and I wanted to win praise from him whenever I played for him.

We kept talking to each other after every over and Imran repeated the need for attacking at the right time. When I got into the eighties, the off spinner Peter Taylor came on and Imran walked down to me to say: 'I know you want to hit him, but just block him and pick up the runs steadily.' He flighted his second delivery and I hit him over long-on for a big six. Imran wasn't too impressed: 'Great shot! But you were lucky – don't forget your hundred is there for you!' Even when I reached my century he was there to temper my joy with caution, telling me to stay there, to keep playing sensibly. Eventually I was bowled, and Imran fol-lowed the same way, but we had helped save the match and I was very proud. Imran had batted for more than eight hours, double my time at the crease, and I can't imagine how tired he must have felt. I was shattered, I wasn't used to the physical or mental demands of playing a long innings, yet there was Imran, at the age of thirty-seven, leading by example hour after hour.

So I picked up the man of the match award for the second Test in a row, and with the last one at Sydney ruined by rain I was also named Pakistan's man of the series. That was a landmark tour for me. I loved playing in Australia, especially in night cricket, and it was fantastic to be able to compete respectably against such a good Australian side in both one-dayers and Tests. I felt I was repaying the faith in me shown by Imran, and it meant a lot to do well in front of my seniors, including Javed Miandad who had backed my potential five years earlier. Many press pundits were now calling me the world's best all-rounder, and certainly Imran continued to agree, but I couldn't accept that. Batting was too demanding for me to be consistent in the way that Ian Botham and Imran had been for so long, and I felt that my bowling was easily my strongest weapon. The media attention was very gratifying, though, on that Australian tour, and I was now mature enough to realise that you need to enjoy the acclaim on your good days. Accept it when you're the centre of attention, because the bad days will always turn up, and you'll be left brooding with no one wanting to interview you.

My continued improvement wasn't the only reason why Pakistan could now be genuinely optimistic about the future. We had unearthed two other young bowlers who clearly had the quality to be part of the scene for years to come. Both Mushtaq Ahmed and Waqar Younis toured for the first time with us on the Australia trip, and although they didn't take many wickets, they gave enough indications that they would become matchwinners. From now on my career would be linked to that of Waqar Younis as we became such a successful opening pair of fast bowlers. Just like myself, Waqar seemed to come from nowhere, but he was much more rounded a bowler than I was when he came into the Pakistan side. He had it all – reverse swing, great pace, the yorker, and a strong physique. I'd seen him bowling in the nets at the Gaddafi Stadium in Lahore, and I thought, 'He's quick, very impressive.' The following day I was watching a local cup game on television at Imran's home and when Waqar came on to bowl I told him to have a good look. Imran was as impressed as me, and the following day Waqar was summoned to the Pakistan senior camp. He made his Test debut in the series against India towards the end of 1989, and a great international career was launched.

He was all over the place when he first came into the side, but that raw talent was there. You can't coach sheer pace into someone, and Waqar had it. He was very self-sufficient and mature for his age, probably due to the four years he spent at boarding school in Sharjah, so he seemed to have no difficulty making the leap from promising young bowler to established star at such a young age. Imran worked hard with him, smoothing off the rough edges but almost everything was in place when he came to his first senior camp. It was interesting to see Imran keep his distance socially from Waqar. The captain seemed happier to spend time with me away from cricket, possibly because we shared the same sense of humour and I gave him his own space. In contrast, Waqar was an aggressive character even as a teenager, with no signs of shyness. He wanted success hungrily.

When the chance came to play county cricket in 1990, he grabbed it. Imran had recommended him strongly to his former county colleague Ian Greig, who was now the captain of Surrey, and he made an immediate, devastating impression. His first game was against Lancashire and I took him out to dinner the night before. He was so excited about the prospect of playing in England and absolutely determined to do well. He did. He blasted out batsmen with sheer pace and late swing. Over the next two seasons a new term came into English cricket – 'Waqared', meaning the late, inswinging yorker that either breaks a toe or smashes into the middle and leg stumps. Everybody kept asking me about this phenomenal new Pakistani bowler in 1990, and I kept repeating he would be a star for years to come. Although we've had our ups and downs, he has been a great help to my international career because it's terrific to have someone so dangerous firing away at the other end. We respect each other's ability and our professional rivalry is so strong that if he takes four wickets I want five, and so on. That can only benefit our team.

Mushtaq Ahmed was just nineteen when he was flown out to replace the great leg spinner Abdul Qadir at the start of that 1989/90 tour, when Abdul damaged a finger. I would say that Abdul remains the better bowler of the two, but time is still on Mushy's side. When I batted against Abdul in the nets, I couldn't pick him at all. He had all the variations, but also the gift of patience, which is vital for a leg spinner. Abdul didn't try to bowl a different ball every over, he seemed to have the knack of using the googly or the top spinner at the right time. Mushy, on the other hand, has always been impetuous, trying too much then bowling the googly too often. Sometimes he has been negated by the batsmen playing him like an off spinner, due to his over-reliance on the googly. He is excitable and a great trier, and he has given the Pakistan attack variety and bubbling enthusiasm throughout the nineties. He is great for the team, an aggressive, happy character who'l bowl all day for you.

So, a strong Pakistan unit was beginning to take shape at the start of the nineties. Some others were also gaining valuable experience of English conditions, and over the next couple of years I'd be joined in England by Salim Malik at Essex, Aqib Javed at Hampshire, and Mushtaq at Somerset. A few also played in the leagues, so we were finding out how to play in a place that offered different challenges to Pakistan domestic cricket. We were very lucky, I agree, and I'm sure it helped us do so well in the Test series we won in England in 1992 and 1996.

Before I rejoined Lancashire for the 1990 season, I had to get my troublesome groin sorted out. This injury had dragged on for two years, and it kept flaring up. Towards the end of the tour to Australia I was having three injections a day, and I was very worried about the long-term effects. The medical experts told me that I pivoted too early in my delivery stride, putting too much pressure on the left side of my groin. A major operation was necessary. I had to stay on in Australia when our tour ended, and the operation was performed in a small mining town in Tasmania called Queenstown, four hours drive from Hobart. I had to go there because the recommended groin specialist was working in the local hospital. The feeling was that he was the best around, so that was good enough for me.

Then followed a prolonged period of recuperation, first in Queenstown, then in the rather more cosmopolitan city of Sydney, before my return to Pakistan. The operation was a success in the long run, but it took some time before I was fully fit and back to my best for Lancashire. My body wasn't strong enough to stand up to a great amount of championship cricket that season, but I hope I made amends in the one-day matches. We were tremendous in one-day cricket in 1990, losing just four out of twenty-eight matches. For the first time, a county won the Benson and Hedges Cup and the NatWest Trophy in the same season, and we also finished second in the Sunday League.

I'll never forget the B and H final, my first at Lord's. The lads had told me it would be a fantastic occasion, but I wasn't ready for it. The whole county seemed to be involved. It was nice getting measured up for a couple of suits, driving down with the whole team in a smart coach, and seeing how excited all the administrative staff were. The red rose symbol seemed to be everywhere, and I was astonished to see so many spectators in a queue that stretched all the way back to our hotel, two hundred yards from the famous Grace Gates at Lord's. When we walked onto the ground for practice, the chants of 'Lancashire! Lancashire!' went up, and I had a tingle down the spine. This really was a big occasion, and I was going to enjoy my day out. I had no fear of failure. I was certain the atmosphere would help me do well. We were playing Worcestershire, a team of great talent and experience, county champions for the previous two seasons but still without a win in a Lord's final.

We batted first and after a middle-order slump I smacked a quick twenty-eight, including two big sixes, the second one particularly enjoyable. It landed high up on the pavilion balcony and I was really fired up by the roars of our supporters. This was a special day and I was certain it would get better. I was first change, and when I came on I was really snorting and pawing the ground, desperate to get at them. The crowd were chanting my name and it really geed me up. Neil Fairbrother has told me that he's never seen me run in so fast as I did that day. Off my second ball, Tim Curtis went for the cut and was caught behind. Our supporters went berserk and all I can remember is my team-mates clambering all over me. Now for Graeme Hick. This match had been built up as an individual contest between me and the new great hope of English cricket, the batsman set to score stacks of runs when he qualified to play international cricket the following year. Well, I was determined that he wouldn't win this particular battle. I bowled a bouncer at him straight away, just to let him know I wouldn't be overawed, and in my eagerness I slipped. After dusting myself down, I roared in and just missed his leg stump with a rapid yorker. I was getting my range now, and the next ball he nicked to our keeper, Warren Hegg. I sprinted past the batsman to congratulate Warren, and even in my moment of triumph I was aware of the noise. I hadn't experienced a sound as intense as that, and I just soared away on adrenalin.

We won the cup easily. I took 3 for 30, and although some thought I might have picked up the Gold Award, I wasn't bothered about that, and good luck to Mike Watkinson for making top score in the match and taking two cheap wickets. It was more important to start repaying the faith Lancashire had expressed in me three years earlier. No matter how well I did for Pakistan I have always been determined to give of my best for my county, and that first Lord's victory will remain one of the happiest memories of my career. That night we went to Stringfellows, the night-club, and as all my team-mates mixed with their wives and girlfriends, including me in all the celebrations, I felt very emotional and proud.

It just wasn't the same special experience for me when we returned to Lord's six weeks later to lift the NatWest Trophy. I'm sure that's because the feeling wasn't novel any more. It was fun to win, of course, but not as stimulating. It may be that the weather had something to do with it – it was cool and damp – and also the result was never in doubt once we had won the toss and put Northants in. Soon they were 39 for 5, every wicket falling to Phil DeFreitas, who bowled ideally in the seamer's conditions, but that killed the game as a spectacle. I wasn't really part of it, although I bowled my full quota of overs cheaply enough. Above all I was pleased for David Hughes, our captain. By this time he was forty-three, not really contributing as a player apart from his excellent fielding, and many were saying that with David in the side we were only playing ten. It was hard to argue with that, although I believe he was a very good captain and there were no other contenders around at that time. The following season, in his twenty-fifth year with Lancashire, David had to stand down on the morning of the Benson and Hedges final, handing over the job to Neil Fairbrother. That was a little messy, and David's dilemma could have been handled with more diplomacy, perhaps a little earlier than on the eve of a Lord's final. I shall always remember him as a captain who knew what he was doing on the field, and someone who made me very welcome when I first arrived at Old Trafford. David Hughes had a lot to do with creating the happy atmosphere I noticed as soon as I joined the club.

I had another good season with Lancashire in 1991, topping the bowling averages and smacking a hundred against Hampshire in my usual style, but I was frustrated yet again by various niggling injuries towards the end of the season, missing some crucial games that might just have brought us the championship. It proved a summer of near-misses for Lancashire as we finished second in the Sunday League and lost in the Benson and Hedges final to Worcestershire. I was particularly happy with the development in my bowling. I felt I could take wickets every time I came on, given the right conditions. I took eleven wickets at Uxbridge in ideal conditions for reverse swing, and when the Hampshire match was drifting to a draw I just sensed it was the right time to bowl. It was hot, the square was very dry, and I swung it so late that four wickets in nine balls brought us an unexpected victory. It seemed to me that I was approaching my peak as a bowler, as long as I could banish my lingering worries about that dodgy left groin and keep clear of the other niggles a fast bowler always encounters.

Having Waqar Younis steaming in at the other end also helped me on Pakistan duty. We blew New Zealand away three-nil, taking thirty-nine wickets between us in the three Tests, and they had great difficulty trying to combat the late inswinging yorkers, apart from that marvellous technician Martin Crowe. He said that in all his career he had never faced fast bowling of the sustained quality that Waqar showed in this particular series. That was a handsome tribute from a great player. We then took another thirty-seven wickets between us in three Tests against the West Indies, a close series that ended one-all. This had been billed as an unofficial world championship (which might have amused the Australians!), and they were stern contests with a lot of pride involved.

We won the first Test in Karachi on a very slow wicket that negated their fast bowlers who liked to dig the ball in to get bounce, but it was ideal for Waqar and myself. Imran had called a team meeting before that Test saying that he was looking for pitches that were soft in the middle and easy-paced on a good length. That would therefore mean that the ball would just sit up slowly from the areas where the West Indian quicks banged it in, and out batsmen wouldn't be troubled by the short, fast delivery aimed at the rib cage, the usual line of attack from Ambrose and the rest. That worked at Karachi, but the groundsman at Faisalabad didn't appear to get Imran's message. The wicket was dry and hard with bounce for their fast bowlers in their favoured business area, and we got hammered by seven wickets.

So to Lahore, and a turning pitch with uneven bounce that broke up after just two days. I took four wickets in five balls in their second innings, and I was surprised to hear afterwards that this had only been done twice before in Test cricket. Everything was right for me, I felt in perfect rhythm, and I would have had a hat-trick if Imran hadn't dropped a dolly. I'd had Gus Logie lbw and Jeff Dujon caught behind off one that lifted and bounced, so I thought hard about the next ball. I told Imran that I was going to bowl Ian Bishop a good-length ball just outside the off-stump from around the wicket. It landed around off-stump, Bishop played across the line, and it dollied up to Imran at mid-on. He put one hand casually to his right, and dropped it. I steeled myself to say nothing to my mentor, the man who had done so much for me, but I stared at him, waiting for the apology. It came from a bashful captain. Another player would have got a rocket from me!

I suppose it didn't matter, because I cleaned up the innings in the next two balls. Usually I managed to get Malcolm Marshall with the yorker from around the wicket as he played away from his body, and this was no exception – clean bowled. Courtney Walsh obliged next ball, having his usual slog to a swinging full-length delivery to be plumb lbw. That was very enjoyable, but it meant more to me when I helped Imran save the game the following day. We batted together for an hour and a half, defying everything that

Malcolm Marshall could hurl at us. Marshall, a great bowler, bowled very rapidly and tried everything, but Imran just wouldn't buckle. He told me to block it out, which didn't suit me, but I loved the fight. It was a great feeling to see Pakistan through to safety, playing in a manner that was against my nature. At this stage in his career Imran wasn't bowling a great deal, saving his energies for his batting, and it wsa a great education to see him build an innings, get his eye in, then go for his shots in one-day matches. When he had to defend to save a game his orthodox, composed technique was hugely impressive and his fighting qualities were contagious.

Pakistan continued to improve in the early nineties. Batsmen like Salim Malik were getting established alongside Javed and Imran, and our young bowlers were turning in impressive figures. We were justifiably confident of winning most of our international matches now, and the 1992 World Cup – to be held in Australia, a place where we all loved to play – was there on the horizon. Yet Pakistan's successes around that time seemed to be viewed with a question mark. The mutterings began during the New Zealand tour to Pakistan towards the end of 1990. After they got home, their manager, Ian Taylor, accused us of doctoring the ball to get extra swing. He also said that their pace bowler, Chris Pringle, had deliberately tampered with the ball during the Faisalabad Test, and as a result he took 7 for 52 and eleven wickets in the game. Chris Pringle never denied the allegation. They also complained about the quality of the umpiring. I thought that was a bit much considering the trouble we'd had on previous tours over there. Steve Dunne is the only good umpire I've seen come out of New Zealand.

The ball-tampering allegations didn't bother us at all. The fact is that no umpire picked us up or made a complaint. Waqar and myself were in good nick, we were too good for their batsmen, and the dry conditions were perfect for swing bowling. We felt we could bowl out any team; there was no need to tamper with the ball. We were always very happy to throw the ball to the umpire at the end of every over so that he could check its condition. John Hampshire and John Holder used to ask to see the ball at randomly selected moments in the series against India the previous year, and they never complained about its state. The West Indies management also alleged ball-tampering during our home series, without any evidence to back up their claims. Quite simply, we could swing the ball more than either the New Zealanders or the West Indians because we were more used to looking after the ball. Wickets in Pakistan are so flat that we have to learn special bowling skills to utilise the climate. Hot weather leads to dusty, dry cricket squares and that helps reverse swing. We have mastered that technique better than other bowlers from other countries, and yet our success has been tainted.

Eyebrows were raised regularly from now on as Waqar and myself continued to take wickets all around the world. It didn't bother me because I was bowling very well and enjoying my success. All I was doing was looking after the ball properly, without the umpires complaining about cheating. Others insisted we were flouting the rules, although without evidence, and that was to be a continuing slur for the next few years. As a result, our relations with England players were to be strained once more.

CHAPTER 6

On Top of the World

NOW I know it's a cliché, but my prayers really were answered when Pakistan won the World Cup in 1992, and I was named man of the final. It was the greatest day of my career when we beat England in the final. I had prayed throughout the tournament for our team and myself to do well. By the time we faced England in front of almost 90,000 in Melbourne, I was convinced we would win, even though they were clear favourites. I'd even persuaded myself that I would dismiss Ian Botham for nought to avenge his stupid remarks about my country a few years earlier. That happened sure enough, and I was so inspired that later on in the England innings I was on a hat-trick. It was a wonderful day for our people, for a young country, and for our supporters all over the world. If I ever experience anything quite so memorable again in my career, I'll be very fortunate.

And yet the tournament started so badly for us. Before a game had been played we lost Waqar Younis to a stress fracture of the back, sustained in the nets in Australia. He went home for surgery and we just shrugged it off; there was no point in feeling sorry for ourselves, we would work even harder to surmount this loss. And we really did work. There was no particular pressure from our management to step up our training, but we all did so voluntarily. We just felt that Australian conditions and that special atmosphere of night cricket would lift us, and that we'd get stronger the longer we stayed in the competition. My aim was to be the outstanding player of the World Cup because I believed I had proved with

Lancashire that I was a big-occasion cricketer. If I played to my potential, the team would also do well, so I trained even harder. Once we got to Australia I'd bowl around three hours a day, practice my fielding for half an hour, then run twelve laps of the ground. Nothing was left to chance, I wouldn't be offering a lack of physical fitness as an excuse for failure. Not that I expected failure.

We were fortified by the prayers of the Pakistan people to back up our own devotions during that period. We were now in Ramadan, that precious month for Muslims. Sometimes it falls from mid-February onwards, at other times it's March into April, but it's the time of year when everything closes down in Pakistan and we pray and fast. During Ramadan, Muslims can eat until five in the morning, then fast till six at night, and pray several times a day. It's designed to get your dietary system cleansed after eleven months of eating, to do something for your God, to test your faith. Muslims pray up to three hours a day during Ramadan, and we knew from phone calls back home to our families just how much we were in the prayers of our Muslim community. That gave us extra strength and incentive. In my time in the Pakistan side only Anil Dalpat – a Hindu – wasn't a Muslim, and we prayed five times a day when we were in Australia. We were exempt from fasting because of our training and the need to sustain the body's strength, but we'd gather at five in the morning to pray, followed by afternoon prayers at one, three, six, and then nine o'clock.

The prayers were led by Javed Miandad, something that might surprise those non-Muslims who have doubted his character over the years! I also haven't always been on the best of terms with Javed – too often he has been excitable on the pitch, contributing to the build-up of extra tension between the opposition and ourselves. Having said that, he was a very effective and devout leader in those prayer sesssions. It's always been very important to me to pray to my God, to gain strength for hard work. It wasn't a case of asking for a stack of wickets and runs, but praying for the dedication to enable you to do well. I believed that if you did the hard work, you would eventually be rewarded – not the next day, or the next week, but possibly the next year. There is no timescale involved. This religious bonding is important in Pakistan sides.

There's often been a lack of self-discipline. We lack that consistent steeliness of the Australians or the South Africans, but when we have to it together it's usually been because we have prayed together regularly, knowing that our God was working for us. It happened in Australia in 1997 when we won the World Series tournament under my captaincy, beating West Indies and Australia without many injured regulars. I was leading a very young side, but we were inspired by Ramadan. Some of the younger players insisted on fasting, even though they were exempt, but the result was a gritty team performance that surprised outsiders. I attribute some of that success to our religious convictions.

Yet I say again, we were a shambles in the early games of that 1992 World Cup. We were bowled out for seventy-four by England at Adelaide, and rain saved us. The point we got from that non-result got us into the semi-finals. West Indies thrashed us by ten wickets, India and South Africa beat us comfortably, and still Imran kept insisting we'd win the World Cup. What's more, I believed him. It was a long competition, lasting a month, with exhausting amounts of travel involved as all sides zig-zagged across Australia and New Zealand, and there was a definite danger of peaking too early.

England had started impressively. They had some vastly experienced players and a number of all-rounders who were one-day specialists, but some of their players were coming towards the end of their careers and Imran was convinced they'd run out of steam. So was I. Seven days before the final I was finally certain we would win the trophy. We had beaten New Zealand in Christchurch, but had to wait a few hours to see if West Indies could beat Australia in Melbourne. Australia had no chance of qualifying for the semi-finals, but they could get us through at the West Indies' expense if they won in Melbourne. We sat in our hotel rooms in Christchurch willing Australia to do it, and when they triumphed we went mad. We started dancing around, with music from a tape recorder blaring down the corridor. That night, when we went out for dinner, I was so excited that I asked our taxi driver for a piece of paper and a pen. On it I wrote: 'March 18, 1992. Pakistan WILL win the World Cup. Wasim Akram.' I wonder if that cabbie still has that scrap of paper?

We didn't fear any of the sides left in the semis now, we just felt that the tide was running our way. Our opponents were New Zealand, who had surprised many by getting so far. Yet we always do well against them and the capacity partisan crowd of 32,000 at Auckland helped lift us even further. We also unveiled a new young star at the perfect time. Inzamam-ul-Haq was just twenty-one and he had come into the one-day team in Sri Lanka a few months earlier, making an immediate impression with two classy centuries. Waqar and Mushtaq Ahmed, who played with him for UBL, had been singing his praises to us and as soon as Imran saw him in the nets he said he was the best batsman in Pakistan. He had a habit of being right with extravagant statements like that, and he didn't retract his comment, even when Inzy failed in the early World Cup rounds. Imran liked to look at the batsman's technique first, before he made any more judgements, and he was immediately impressed by Inzy because he didn't hit the ball in the air and was a very accomplished driver and cutter (safe shots in Imran's opinion). His timing was superb, and his eye so sharp that he looked a wonderful player in the nets, whipping our inswingers through mid-wicket with insolent grace. Imran was convinced in no time at all: Inzy was going to the World Cup.

He saved his best for the crucial games. In the Auckland semi-final we started slowly, chasing 262 in fifty overs. Imran, going in at number three, got bogged down, and when Inzy went in we needed another 123 at eight an over. The home supporters were convinced they were off to Melbourne for the final, but our young genius had other ideas. He batted amazingly, making sixty off thirty-seven balls, hitting cleanly in textbook style and looking so calm. Javed, using all his experience, blocked one end and gave the strike to Inzy, telling him to go with the flow. Then the old head was used to guide us home near the end and we won by four wickets with an over to spare.

We didn't care who we played in the final. It turned out to be England, after rain brought a farcical end to the other semi in Sydney when it looked as though South Africa might squeeze home. A shower adjusted South Africa's target to twenty-one runs off one ball, which was a joke, but the rules were in place at the start of the tournament. Everybody complained about the rain reg-

ulations, but hardly a player seemed to have grasped their significance until it was too late. I include the Pakistan camp in this cate-
gory! It was a shame for South Africa, I agree, but the demands of
worldwide television meant the games had to be played within a
certain period of time, so some sort of equation was needed to get
them finished in a window of maximum exposure.

So it was England in the final. Like us, they hadn't ever won the
trophy, and for some of their most experienced players like
Graham Gooch, Ian Botham and Allan Lamb, it would be their last
chance. In any other circumstances I'd be cheering on my good
friend and Lancashire team-mate Neil Fairbrother, but this time he
was the opposition and I was a proud Pakistani determined to put
one over on Neil, one of the best one-day batsmen in the world. On
the morning of the final I got up around ten o'clock, feeling
refreshed after a good night's sleep. It had been a good idea to take
a light sleeping pill. I prayed in my room, had a light breakfast, and
joined the boys for practice, which went superbly. I felt I wasn't
losing any strength, I was just floating. There was no doubt in my
mind that I was going to do well, that the atmosphere would bring
out the best in me. It was just like my first appearance for
Lancashire in a Lord's final: I wanted to seize the limelight and
dominate the opposition. England were the favourites, understandably because of their experience and because you never knew what
side of the bed our team would get out of. We could be brilliant
one day and a shambles the next, as we had proved so far in this
competition. But Imran's team talk that day was pitched perfectly.
He was wearing a T-shirt with a tiger on the front, and he pointed
to it saying: 'We're going to fight like cornered tigers, boys, they
won't beat us.' You could see everyone in the room growing in
stature and self-belief. We just couldn't believe that England would
be as motivated as us, with the prayers of millions of Muslims willing us on.

After winning the toss and deciding to bat, we made a bad start;
we lost early wickets, then Imran and Javed batted slowly. At one
stage Imran scored just nine in sixteen overs and I was mystified.
As the overs ticked away I started to panic. We all knew that his
tactic when batting in such games is to occupy the crease for a long
time, then increase the tempo later on with the luxury of wickets in

hand, but this was surely taking caution too far. If he had been caught by Gooch off a skier we would have been in trouble, because a lot of overs had been used up by then – we were only 70 for 2 at the halfway mark – but he survived and started to play shots. Inzamam then came in to blaze away, I smashed thirty-three off eighteen balls, and we got to 249 for 6 in our fifty overs, with the last twenty bringing us 153 runs. I had been promoted up the order ahead of batsmen of the calibre of Ijaz Ahmed and Salim Malik, and I knew what I had to do.

England looked shattered towards the end of our innings. Their fielding flagged on the vast playing area of the MCG and only Derek Pringle among their bowlers kept the right line as we laid about them. I felt they were gone before we bowled a ball, and we were so relaxed and positive in between the innings. Imran spoke again to us before we went out to field: 'Don't forget, we fight like cornered tigers,' he said. 'Everyone's praying for us back home, we mustn't let them down.' After he spoke we all hugged each other in the dressing-room. We just couldn't wait to get at England. Our intensity was overwhelming.

We knew it was vital quickly to separate the opening pair of Gooch and Botham, two very dangerous players. Botham in particular could have altered the shape of the game in just ten overs or so, as he had proved already in the competition, and I got him for nought in my first over! He wasn't happy with the decision that saw him caught behind, and he stood there in disbelief. I couldn't understand what he was on about because we all went up for the appeal when the ball brushed his glove. It was a big 'out', and the TV replay supported umpire Aldridge. Botham was even less happy at being sent on his way with some choice words from our close fielders. None of us had forgotten his contemptuous remarks about Pakistan, or that he clearly thought little of us. Perhaps Aamir Sohail went a bit too far with his language. He speaks English very well and realised that there was no point in swearing at Botham in Urdu, so he gave him the sort of volley he would understand, the kind of message Botham had handed out to our batsmen in the past when he was still a top player.

Graeme Hick, the next man in, was obviously a dangerous batsman who would thrive on the fact that we couldn't bounce him due

My mother was responsible for giving me and my brothers and sister an enjoyable, though strict, upbringing. I am sitting second from the right, with Nadeem and my mother with Sofia on the left, and Naeem on the far right. (Wasim Akram)

Above My father has been wonderfully supportive throughout my life. This is my wedding day in 1993. (Wasim Akram)

Left My wife Huma and I have known each other for ten years. She is a qualified hypnotherapist and psychotherapist and has helped me to be mentally strong throughout my career. (Wasim Akram)

Winning the 1992 World Cup was one of the most spectacular moments in my career. We were led to victory by my friend and mentor, Imran Khan. (Patrick Eagar)

I haven't always been on the best of terms with Javed Miandad but when you win the World Cup, nothing else seems important. (Allsport)

Below This is the famous World Cup trophy. I think my smile says it all. (Allsport)

Bowling has always been my passion. All those hours in the nets have really been worth while. (Empics)

to the one-day regulations, but Mushtaq Ahmed was equal to the challenge. He completely outwitted Hick with the googly, pinning him lbw on the back foot, and then he got the key wicket, that of Graham Gooch. We had great respect for Gooch. He had the temperament that relishes responsibility and the range of strokes that could tame any attack, but Mushy stood up to him, bowling aggressively. Finally Gooch top-edged a sweep and our hearts were in our mouths as the ball hung in the air. Underneath it was the team's worst fielder, Aqib Javed, running in full tilt from long leg. Yet he took it one-handed to our great joy and that was a hammer blow to England. They weren't finished, though, because Lamb and Fairbrother started to play very well. They had added seventy-two at five an over when I suggested to Imran that it might be an idea to give me a go for a couple of overs. They were down to just a hundred for victory with six wickets in hand and a comfortable rate of six an over. We needed wickets. 'Come on, Was,' my captain said. 'Do it for us, get us some wickets.'

It was a good time for me to be bowling again. It was humid and the ball was reversing from the Pavilion End, so I chose to bowl at that end. With white balls being used at both ends, there was every chance of it swinging in the humidity because it was only seventeen overs old. Neil Fairbrother told me afterwards that he said to Lamb, 'Don't do anything flashy against Was, just see him off', so he was aware that England held the initiative. They could afford to block me and still have enough overs left to win. After my first ball of this new spell I decided to go around the wicket to the right-handed Lamb. I was looking to get the ball to dip in, then move alway late. That's exactly what happened with my first delivery: it swung in, left Lamb off the pitch, and hit off-stump as he shaped to play the on-drive. I ran past Lamb and high-fived everyone who could get near to me.

Then Chris Lewis came in, a batsman I knew would try to get on to the front foot against me. Imran said: 'Bowl a good-length ball that'll come into him. He'll be looking for the yorker, so give him something he won't be expecting.' The ball pitched outside the off-stump, jagged back in, and squeezed through a tiny gap to hit the top of the stump. Lewis couldn't blame himself for that; he had everything covered but the ball came back just far enough. So now

I was on a hat-trick, though I had to wait to the start of my next over. The man I had to face was my old friend, Neil Fairbrother, and afterwards he told me that he was convinced I was going to bowl him a big inswinger, so he just set out to block me. Unfortunately, in my haste to get at Neil I bowled a no-ball. That would have been too much to ask – getting a hat-trick in a World Cup Final! Neil could still have done it for them, I suppose, but he lacked support, and when he was seventh out we were home and I could savour the atmosphere and the feeling of elation. It was appropriate that Imran took the final wicket because he had done so much for the careers of many of us there, particularly mine. When that wicket fell, we all went down on our knees to thank our God. With security at the MCG so tight, none of the crowd could get on to the playing surface, so we could enjoy the moment and hug each other.

We were still on a high when Imran made his famous speech from the podium, words that alienated many of our players later on. Apparently he didn't mention our efforts, but talked about what victory meant to him and dedicated his success to his late mother, in whose memory he had pledged to build a cancer hospital for the poor people of Pakistan. His words meant nothing to us at the time because we weren't listening to him. We were far too excited as we hugged each other, chattering away about how we had done it. I don't blame Imran for forgetting to mention the boys. You can't prepare a comprehensive speech for such a hugely emotional moment with the eyes of millions of cricket fans on you as it's beamed live into television sets all over the world. Even such a sophisticated, intelligent man as Imran was bound to talk off the top of his head, without weighing the significance of his words. He had always been very generous in praising his players, supporting their careers, and encouraging them to strive to greater heights, and I wasn't put out at all when his words were read out in the cold light of day. I can't imagine what I would have babbled if I'd been Pakistan's captain that evening!

Sadly, that speech backfired on Imran and led to a chain of events that saw him stand down as captain for our tour to England, which started six weeks later. Even before the World Cup some of the boys had been getting fed up with his obsession with the cancer hospital. It was a wonderful aim, to create a hospital where the poor of Pakistan could be treated for cancer free of charge, Imran had taken to accepting invitations to functions and guaranteeing that the rest of his players would also be there, with all the money going to the hospital fund. Some of the guys felt they were being taken for granted and didn't see why they should travel long distances, listen to speeches, and get paid nothing. No one denied that it ws a marvellous cause – heaven knows, our country needed a cancer hospital – but some of our players were quite poor themselves, and they could have done with some extra money. Others had their own personal charities, but found that the demands from Imran meant they had no time to spare for them. The feeling spread that Imran was being tactless, taking us for granted, that a percentage from these official functions should go to the hospital and perhaps seventy per cent to the players.

Things came to a head on the stopover in Singapore as we travelled home from Melbourne. A charity dinner raised a lot of money and it all went to the hospital fund. That was the last straw for most of the players. We had a meeting and the majority opinion was that we should do no more for Imran's charity. When the next function was held in Lahore, no Pakistan player turned up. Imran then declared himself unavailable for the England tour, saying he had a shoulder injury. He was, after all, now thirty-nine, and at that advanced stage of his career the niggling injuries do pile up. But I think he judged the situation correctly. He had lost his hold over the players, forfeited a little respect. Without a doubt he was aware that he might have difficulty motivating the boys again, so soon after they had indicated their displeasure, so it made sense for him to bow out on a high note, avoiding the risk of unpleasantness. He was right to do so, because some of the boys definitely thought he had been too dictatorial, and when you've won a World Cup you tend to have a little more confidence in expressing your views, even to an idol such as Imran Khan.

I didn't hold such strong views about the matter, and I would have been more than happy to play under Imran in England. The money we missed out on didn't bother me, because I was well paid, but I could see that Imran might have handled the situation a little more tactfully. I've often wondered if Imran would have defused the tension between the two sides during that tempestuous tour to England in 1992 as we fought tooth and nail under the volatile leadership of Javed Miandad. Perhaps the loss of some credibility in his players' eyes might have reduced Imran's effectiveness as a calming influence. We shall never know.

Yet no one should ever diminish Imran's role in our victory in the 1992 World Cup. The following day I was the centre of media attention having won the man of the match award, and I lapped up the interest shown in me. It was our captain, though, who had guided many of our careers and kept faith in us a month before when we were so awful. We won just one of our first five games in the early rounds, but he reiterated that we'd come good at the right time. Our victory stemmed from a positive approach. The solid experience of Imran and Javed allowed us to blaze away with the bat, while we attacked when we bowled. England's team was packed with medium-pacers who looked to bowl line and length with little imagination. That was the established formula for one-day cricket, but the old order was changing and England didn't see it. We bowled them out on a good pitch with a combination of speed, swing, and leg spin. It was great to see the leggies of Mushtaq take three important wickets at a time when many believed that this sort of bowling was a luxury in the one-day format. Any type of bowling which takes wickets quickly is not a luxury, and that's why England were reduced to 69 for 4. In the last couple of years leading up to the World Cup, we had won several one-day games by taking ten wickets cheaply instead of trying just to defend a low total. We had the attacking bowlers to do that, and Imran gave us the positive philosophy to go for broke. We may have been erratic, but we were exciting to watch because you never knew if we were in for an inspired day. In 1996 Sri Lanka lifted the World Cup by approaching one-day cricket in the same way, while England remained stuck in a conventional rut, still waiting to win the trophy after six attempts and three defeats in the final. Sri Lanka proved to be quick learners, unlike England, the originators of the one-day game.

We had no doubts what our victory meant to the Pakistan nation, but before we could experience our homecoming reception we went to Saudi Arabia for a pilgrimage to Mecca to give thanks for our famous victory. After flying into Karachi airport, we spent three hours under tight security before leaving for Mecca. We had two days there, an inspirational time for us. We visited Mecca at night, washed, had our hair cut, changed into religious clothes, and prayed. More than a million Muslims were in Mecca at the same time, but our privacy wasn't invaded. We also visited Madina, where the prophet Mohammad is buried. It was a memorable couple of days, a necessary part of our celebrations. The we flew back to Lahore in our prime minister's plane. The scene at the airport was astonishing. At least 10,000 officials were on the tarmac to greet us when we came down the steps of the plane. We all made a bee-line for one particular man who had come to greet us – Waqar Younis. He was in tears, and I can only imagine what he must have been feeling as I too cried with him. It must have been so hard for him knowing that only his back injury prevented him from being on the field with us just a few days earlier. I just hope he gets the chance to play in a World Cup Final before he retires.

Then it was time to meet our people. We were due at the Pearl Inter-Continental Hotel for another function, usually a twenty-minute drive from Lahore airport. It took six hours that day. The crowds had started lining up the night before, ready for our arrival at nine in the morning. The heat was intense and many were fainting. I felt goosebumps of excitement as many tried to kiss my hands and threw fruit as we passed slowly by in the motorcade. Finally, hours later, I managed to get home to my family. They hugged me joyfully, put flowers around my neck, and told me they were so proud. This was four days after the final, but I still hadn't come down to earth. I couldn't sleep for excitement that night, so I got up and went to visit some of my friends. Their simple expressions of joy touched me greatly and brought home to me just what we had achieved for our country. My prayers, and those of the world's Muslim communities had been answered.

When India won the World Cup in 1983 I was very envious, especially as we had lost in the semi-finals. I read about the massive celebrations throughout their land, and hoped one day that we would enjoy the same experience. I still feel a tingle of pride and excitement every time I think about the 1992 World Cup, or if anyone mentions it to me. It will never be forgotten by the Pakistani people. Three years later on our tour to Zimbabwe, a Muslim who lived in Harare invited a few of the players over to his house for dinner. As soon as we walked in he asked us to sit down, and then switched on the video of that memorable game. I shall never tire of watching it.

CHAPTER 7

England's Bad Losers

OUR 1992 tour to England featured some magnificent cricket, mostly from our side. We won the series two-one to record our fourth successive win over England, and fair-minded cricket supporters acknowledged that we played very entertainingly, always going out for a win even when we played one of the counties in-between Tests. Yet our triumphant tour ended with us being branded as cheats. With those allegations coming from the England camp, backed up by some irresponsible sections of the tabloid press, the atmosphere was very poisonous by the time we flew home at the end of August.

We were accused of systematically tampering with the ball throughout the summer, gaining an unfair advantage for our swing bowlers, Waqar and myself. It did not seem to matter that at no stage did any of the umpires pick us up over the state of the ball, or any complaint come from the match referees, or any of the allegations get substantiated. There had to be good reasons why England kept collapsing so spectacularly against our fast bowlers. That was it: we weren't any better, they just got away with doctoring the ball and the authorities turned a blind eye. A convenient excuse for those who didn't seem to grasp that the game had moved on, that reverse swing was an accepted, legitimate technique used by fast bowlers in other parts of the world where you have to work hard for your wickets.

I had grown up thinking that English sportsmen were good losers, keeping the stiff upper lip when things didn't go their way on the pitch, willing to congratulate the victorious opposition. That was what I was told as I learned to speak the language at my school in Lahore. When I first played in England I soon came to appreciate the good things about English cricket. I liked the cricketers, they did seem sporting in defeat and modest in victory. That was only in county cricket though. When they played for England againt Pakistan their attitude changed, and I could tell they believed we were a bunch of cheats. The old scars from 1987 hadn't really healed by the time we came to England five years later, and there were also some new ones from the World Cup Final just a few weeks earlier. It rankled with them that we had beaten them, and we were aware that they'd been muttering about how I'd managed to swing the ball so prodigiously during my second spell. So here we were again, facing up to one another too quickly with no time for tempers to cool.

There's no doubt that Pakistani cricketers of my generation have raised their game when they tour England. That's partly due to the tradition of playing in England, the home of cricket, with its excellent facilities and ease of travel and communication. We also get a lot of strength from our noisy and enthusiastic supporters who live there. We get a great kick out of beating England on their home turf, with their umpires. After the amount of stick handed out to our umpires by English tourists, we no longer turn the other cheek when it comes to the defects of certain English arbiters. Dickie Bird's inclination to give 'not outs' was legendary anyway, we had no faith in the reliability of David Constant, and our doubts over Ken Palmer were confirmed in the 1992 Test at Leeds when he failed to give Graham Gooch run out when he was at least three yards out of his crease and not even in the frame on the television action replay. Pakistan continued to press for umpires from a third country, and we were dismayed to discover that, although the ICC had already agreed to the principle of an international panel, they would not be using any for this forthcoming series. A lack of money was given as the reason, yet four referees were flown over to supervise our matches. They found the cash to allow former players to watch the game on television all day in a quiet room, but not to get the best umpires involved. It didn't occur to the ICC that you very rarely need a referee if the players have confidence in an efficient umpire who will ensure fairness and instil discipline by example.

So we didn't expect to have a happy series when we arrived in England, and the usual suspicious activities of the drugs officials at Heathrow airport hardly made us feel welcome. They searched everything for hours and drew a blank, just like in 1987. We knew that we'd be scrutinised very closely on the field for any misdemeanours. Since New Zealand had accused us of ball-tampering two years earlier there had been a lot of whispers about us on the international circuit, but we were determined to ignore the rumours. Waqar and I felt the best way to fight back was to take a stack of wickets, to kick English butt. We were very strong mentally, aware that we were in for a rough passage, but that helped bind us together as a unit. Our team spirit throughout was brilliant on that tour. We were still on a high after winning the World Cup.

The bad feeling that had rumbled on throughout the tour came to a head in August when Allan Lamb went public in a tabloid newspaper alleging that we had tampered with the ball during the one-day international at Lord's. Lamb alleged that he had brought to the umpires' attention the state of the ball at lunchtime, saying that we had doctored it. He said he definitely saw Aqib Javed scratching the ball when we gathered in a huddle at the fall of a wicket, and that the ball was swinging violently when it was just twenty-five overs old. Just to add fuel to the story, Ian Botham rang the press box when the game was over to tip them off that we were in trouble, that the ball had been changed because we had tampered with it. All this just a fortnight after England's team manager, Mickey Stewart, had said to the press after our victory in the Oval Test that he knew how Pakistan's bowlers managed to make the old ball swing so prodigiously, but was unwilling to reveal anything else. The implication was clear: we were cheating and England had to fight us with one hand tied behind their backs. So we had Botham and Lamb feeding stories to the tabloids, even though for years they had made clear their contempt for such newspapers.

It was hard to avoid the frenzy whipped up by the press after that Lord's game. We had managed to keep our strong team spirit together for the whole tour because we knew how well we had played, and it was clear that the vast majority of English fans appreciated our skill. Yet many English players had been moaning and groaning to the umpires throughout the series, trying to find reasons why they were batting so poorly against late swing that occasionally made them look technically inadequate. Once again, there was no rapport at all with a few of the older English players – apart from David Gower who was as usual, the perfect gentlemen – although some of the younger ones, like Mark Ramprakash and Ian Salisbury, were pleasant enough, as well as Lancashire team-mates Michael Atherton and Neil Fairbrother. Othewise, it was like being part of a cold war, with no attempt to be sociable towards us. They were very talkative to the umpires though, behind our backs, and that Lord's one-day international was the culmination of a whispering campaign that just got louder.

That Lord's game was spread over two days due to rain, and the suspicions about us emerged on the Sunday morning as we defended a small total of 204. The ball had got soft surprisingly early, perhaps due to the damp outfield, and several times during that morning session we showed it to the umpires saying it was out of shape. They carried on with it, and Lamb alleged that we were swinging it all over the place when it was only twenty-five to thirty overs old. That's simply incorrect. I've looked at the video of that session, and the ball was seaming around off the pitch; there was no reverse swing. Waqar and I knew that the conditions weren't right for reverse swing, it wasn't dry enough. The umpires kept examining the ball at regular intervals and at lunchtime they told us they were going to change it. We were happy with that, because we couldn't grip it properly and weren't bowling all that well. And yet Lamb says we were swinging it like a boomerang! He was out there batting, so I wondered about his cricketing knowledge when I heard that!

After lunch we bowled much better – with the replacement ball, not the one we had allegedly doctored. England slumped from 172 for 5 to 201 all out with Waqar and myself cleaning up the tail, without the use of reverse swing, just using the dampish conditions to bowl normal swing and seam the ball around at pace; without the ball that had apparently made us so unplayable in the morning session. As for Aqib scratching the ball in the morning session, I remember clearly standing alongside him after he'd bowled Neil Fairbrother's off-stump with an inswinger, and I had the ball in my hand, not Aqib. Lamb was the non-striker and he says that Aqib was tampering with the ball, but I think he was dreaming. I spent some time shining one side on my sleeve, waiting for the new batsman to come in, and then I threw it back to Aqib to bowl at the new batsman. We all knew that with rumours flying around the television cameras would be closely scrutinising us; did Lamb think we'd be so stupid as to cut up the ball in full view of millions of people?

What really fanned the flames was the reaction afterwards of the ICC referee, Deryck Murray. He refused to make any comment, other than confirming that the ball had been changed. That gave our detractors an open goal to aim at. The implication was that the ball had been doctored, whereas out team manager, Intikhab Alam, maintained that it had been changed simply because it had gone out of shape. Few seemed to notice that we actually wanted the ball to be changed throughout the morning session. If we had been messing around with it, wouldn't we have wanted to hang on to it? Under the regulations, that ball would have had to be changed for one of inferior condition if it had been deliberately damaged, yet the replacement ball after lunch was of a similar condition. Surely that meant we were innocent?

Murray knew all this, but his refusal to comment led to allegations along the lines of 'no smoke without fire, you know'. We were amazed and annoyed at his silence. If we were guilty, he should have said so. If not, then clear us. His performance did nothing for the status of the new referees' panel; it suggested that they all just wanted a quiet life, leaving it to the media to conduct investigations. So Allan Lamb, nearing the end of his career, got himself one last pay day and acted as a martyr by standing up for the good name of English cricket against those Pakistani cheats. It was as pathetic as the ruling a few days later from the ICC when they decided the matter closed after an in-depth investigation. But they didn't implicate us or declare us innocent. It was all left in the closet, with many unanswered questions and a cloud over the Pakistan team.

Throughout that 1992 summer we would throw the ball to the

umpires regularly for their inspection, and no one picked us up on anything. The only time the ball was changed was in that Lord's one-dayer. The most experienced umpires, like Dickie Bird and David Shepherd, were very relaxed about it, while the younger ones like Roy Palmer were very keen to keep looking at the ball. That didn't bother us at all. After England's first innings at Leeds, the ball went to the match referee, Clyde Walcott, for its usual inspection, and even though it was 113 overs old he found nothing unusual about its condition. You would have thought that if we were regular tamperers with the ball, we would have tried altering it at some stage during 113 overs, but no. At every interval the ball was examined by the referee and at no stage were we censured. If only Deryck Murray had justified his fee by speaking out at Lord's, the Pakistani players might have been judged differently.

This cloud of suspicion has never really blown away. Allan Lamb's autobiography was cleverly timed to coincide with our 1996 tour to England, while other books have made various accusations. More damagingly, Imran Khan admitted in a book in 1993 that he had used a bottle top on a ball while playing for Sussex, and he then took wickets with that ball after it had been gouged when it started to swing alarmingly. I was amazed at Imran's revelation. I couldn't imagine what sort of state that ball would be in or how he could get away with it with the umpires close at hand. There was also the implication that if the great Imran had done this, then so had his two protégés, Waqar Younis and Wasim Akram. It put an unnecessary strain on us as we continued our careers trying to eradicate that taint.

To Imran, enjoying his retirement, leading a glamorous lifestyle and occasionally writing a cricket article, this probably didn't mean a great deal. To those who admired him so much and gained such inspiration from him, we felt let down. He had never mentioned such a thing when he was our captain, and even though he said he only did it once, for a laugh, at Sussex, the implication was that he and others had done it for Pakistan. That comment led to a joke at my expense when we were playing Warwickshire in a Sunday League match. I was fielding down at long leg and wanted my sweater from the dressing-room. As I looked towards our twelfth man, the Warwickshire captain, Dermot Reeve, came out with a bottle top in his hand and asked, 'Do you want this?' Now Reeve had the reputation of having a smart mouth, and he probably thought it a good joke, but I was furious. After that, until his retirement, Dermot Reeve always got a hot reception from me. I always wanted to bowl when he came in to bat.

So the finger kept on being pointed at Waqar and myself, thanks in part to Deryck Murray's silence and Imran Khan's baffling admission about the bottle top. At no stage in my career has an umpire said, 'Stop that! You're tampering with the ball.' It would be virtually impossible to do that in front of umpires, especially in England where they have become very jumpy about this issue. At various stages we all do little things to help the ball along. When I want it to get drier to aid the reverse swing, I've thrown the ball on the square, into a rough patch. The old convention of throwing the ball on the full toss to a fielder isn't so prevalent now, you throw it on the bounce, hoping that it'll land on the ball's rough side so that it'll swing more. I've taken mud off the seam and raised the seam with my finger, but so has many another bowler. Sometimes, when my grip isn't too good, I'll put mud or earth on the seam and wet my fingers, but I don't call that ball-tampering. Sometimes, the spinner is brought on for a few overs to help the ball eventually reverse swing. He'll bowl into the rough to dry out the ball and eventually the swing bowler will be able to swing it. They're just tricks of the trade.

I still have the ball with which I took 12 for 125, my career best, against Yorkshire in 1993, a ball that was inspected after every over by the umpires. The side I used for the reverse swing isn't badly scuffed at all; the small cuts were caused by the bat and the ball hitting the boundary boards. The smooth side of the ball is an even surface, with no disfigurement. It's the same with the ball I had mounted after taking 8 for 30 and 5 for 17 against Somerset in 1994. That was also scrutinised by the umpire after each over and nothing was said to me. This after the events and accusations of 1992 had ensured that English umpires would now be especially vigilant over alleged ball-tampering.

I'm certain that the English camp tried to catch us out in 1992 because they failed to understand that they had been undermined by a radical new bowling technique. The new art of swing bowling had passed them by and they were found out. They prided themselves on their professionalism, yet couldn't combat this new form of swing bowling. In Pakistan the conventional form of swing bowling was being negated by the dry atmosphere and pitches. The shine would come off the ball very quickly and it wouldn't move in the air, and batsmen were under no pressure. We started to avoid the usual method of keeping one side polished, hoping that would aid the swing. Instead, we kept one side smooth and the other rough. The idea is to weigh down one side of the ball so that it acts as a bias against the other, leading to unexpected and late swing. We would weigh down the smooth side with sweat and spit, earth or mud, so that it would be heavier than the dry, rough side. With the ball hitting the boundary boards or the bat or the rough parts of the square, it's bound to show signs of wear and tear, and that's why we could get reverse swing after forty or fifty overs. So the idea that swing bowlers were dangerous at the start of the innings, with the polish still on the new ball, went out of the window. We needed a contrast in the sides of the ball to get pronounced swing.

The conventional method of delivering the inswinger involved pointing the smooth, polished side to the offside, and for some reason it would swing in. Instead we pointed the damper, heavier side towards leg and it would be dragged in that direction. There is nothing illegal in making one side of the ball heavier with spit or sweat, but it isn't legal when the rough side is gouged to make it lighter and aid reverse swing. If it's working well, you can really get the ball to dart in late – as Waqar showed when he burst on to the English cricket scene in 1990 with those deadly inswinging yorkers. The top batsmen could see the direction of the shiny side and play accordingly, but with reverse swing it became a guessing game. You started to see batsmen being bowled or trapped lbw by deliveries that started outside the off-stump. The key is late swing, which you can only get when the ball is pitched right up at yorker length. The ball has to be losing speed before it starts to swing late, and then the bias in weight against the rough side comes into play.

Control from the bowler is essential – you are meat and drink to the class batsman if you overpitch or aim too much towards legside. Your wrist action has to be strong to impart pace, and you really need to put effort into the delivery when bowling the yorker.

The amount of effort involved in reverse swing means you can't do it all the time, because your spells will then be very short. You can't coast with reverse swing, every ball needs to be up there in yorker territory, although you slip in the occasional orthodox swinging delivery just to keep them guessing. For me, bowling reverse swing around the wicket to a right-hander, I'll start my line at first or second slip, aim for it to duck in around middle and off-stumps, and hope that the batsman has decided to play no stroke to one he believes will pass outside his off-stump. If I aim too straight they can pick me off easily enough as the ball strays down legside. So control is crucial. That means hours of practice in the nets, something I did when I first came to Lancashire when I experimented with different grips and angles.

I can always tell when the conditions favour reverse swing. You can't do it on a cloudy day, or if the wicket is damp. The square has to be dry so that the ball gets roughed up quicker and the shine goes. The Reader ball is preferable to the one made by Duke's, because there is too much lacquer on a Duke's and it doesn't scuff up so quickly. I remember Phil DeFreitas complaining that we opted for the Reader ball when he played with us at Lancashire. He said it was no use to him because he wanted to swing it naturally, as well as use the seam, and why were we doing this just for our overseas players? Well, it wasn't my fault that DeFreitas's mind was closed to the new technique of swing bowling, and the fact that I used to bowl sides out more often than him was surely of relevance. When Lancashire switched to Duke's one season, I still took wickets faster than DeFreitas.

In 1992 we were lucky to win the toss so often for choice of balls; in Tests and one-day internationals the Reader ball was used eight times, the Duke just twice. So that was an advantage to us. So were the wickets in the Tests. Old Trafford, Lord's, and the Oval were dry, and with Edgbaston a rain-affected draw only Headingly turned out to be a typically English, green seamer's pitch. That was the Test we lost, as England outbowled us in conditions that were second nature to them. I got the impression that Graham Gooch and his team coach, Keith Fletcher, hadn't done their homework, failing to notice where Waqar and I picked up the bulk of our wickets in recent series. On dry, flat pitches. So they served up dry, flat pitches.

Amid all the accusations about ball-tampering, we were very grateful to one former England captain who could see the merits of our bowling. Geoffrey Boycott wrote: 'Wasim and Waqar could bowl out our lot with an orange, because they are great bowlers.' We appreciated that. England seemed to have no batting strategy against us in that series. It was soon obvious that the ball would swing around after forty or so overs, but they hadn't worked out how to combat it. A player like Martin Crowe had managed that in a recent series against us by blocking the reverse swing, playing forcing strokes when we overpitched, and aiming to tire us out by batting for a long time. I got the feeling that little work was being done in the nets on how to play reverse swing, probably because no one could bowl it. So they kept collapsing and then moaning about our methods. At the end of the Test they'd go back to their counties, reassemble in ten days' time, and still have no idea how to bat against reverse swing. And eventually they got the press to start a witch-hunt.

Test matches are usually played on flat pitches and you have to learn new ways of dismissing good batsmen. Pakistan had proved themselves to be innovators, but we had developed the technique of reverse swing through hard work, dedicated practice, and fitness. England failed to learn how to cope with it as batsmen or to adopt it as bowlers. It was no mystery; I had shown the boys at Old Trafford how to do it in previous years, but nobody had followed through on it. Since then my Lancashire team-mates Ian Austin and Peter Martin have become exponents of the art, and Darren Gough and Chris Lewis have used reverse swing when playing for England. So it looks as if they're catching up at last. Yet there was no acknowledgement of our bowling skills at the end of the Oval Test in 1992, just a heavy hint from Mickey Stewart that we'd been cheating all summer. Coming from the team manager, that was tantamount to saying that his players felt the same way.

They ought to have looked at their own batting defects instead. At the Oval England went from 182 for 3 to 207 all out, and in the second innings from 153 for 5 to 174 all out, to lose in just over three days on an ideal batting surface. At Lord's they lost their last six wickets for forty-two and thirty-eight runs respectively, and in the Leeds Test their last eight wickets went for twenty-eight in the first innings. It became a case of 'If Waqar doesn't get them, Wasim will', and I believe that much of this batting was inept and spineless. Those five spectacular collapses added up to 221 runs for the loss of thirty-six wickets, of which Waqar and I claimed twenty-four, and it was clear England were shattered, that another failure was in the back of their minds. Instead of fighting it out, they kept buckling, looking to blur the issue with ball-tampering innuendos.

That tour capped a great year for me, after Pakistan's success in the World Cup. I didn't know until years later that my eighty-two wickets on the England tour were the most by a tourist since 1964, and that was after missing some early games and the first Test with a stress fracture of the shin. Waqar was also struggling for full fitness after his recent serious back injury, but our medical back-up was excellent. By the time I got to the Oval I felt in great form, as if I could get a wicket every delivery. Two wickets I picked up at the Oval stay particularly in my memory, and each time Derek Pringle was the unlucky batsman: from over the wicket I hit his off-stump with one that pitched on leg, and then I went around the wicket to hit off-stump with one that pitched on middle and squared him up. They were almost unplayable. In the Leeds Test I was very happy with the one that bowled Mike Atherton. He and Graham Gooch had built an excellent opening partnership when I bowled him off-stump, beating him on the outside with what was, in effect, a fast leg-break. It had to be a good delivery to bowl Athers when he's on seventy-six and digging in for another Test hundred, and I ribbed him about it for some time afterwards.

That was the only wicket I picked up in that Leeds Test, and it was the worst I bowled all summer. I kept beating the bat with bounce and outswing, and many experts said how unlucky I'd been, but I was dumb. I should have taken steps to curb the swing. I ought to have bowled around the wicket to the right-hander, as I did at the Oval, thereby cutting down on the swing. Instead, I got carried away at Leeds, angry that I kept passing the bat on the outside, but not figuring out why. It was a harsh reminder to me that you have to think for yourself in Test cricket, and be flexible.

Waqar and I took forty-three wickets out of seventy-one in that Test series, but it was a partnership with the bat that gave us particular pleasure, when we hung on at Lord's to scrape a win by two wickets. England should have beaten us on that tense fourth evening when our batsman panicked. We only needed 138 to win, but when I walked in we were 62 for 5. Soon it was 68 for 6, with Ian Salisbury turning his leg-breaks sharply. I told myself I had to do what Imran always advised in these circumstances and block it. That was our only chance of winning, yet we kept losing wickets, and when Waqar joined me we were 95 for 8. I hadn't given up hope, though. Waqar had shown his batting capabilities in a few one-day internationals for us. He was rash, lacking concentration, but could hit the ball a long way. Above all, he has always been a very tough competitor and could be relied on to guts it out. Chris Lewis, who had bowled brilliantly, was now out on his feet, and neither Botham or DeFreitas could bowl through injury. Although Salisbury was bowling well, it suited me to face him because left-handers can negate leggies, and so it proved. I just blocked him while Waqar clubbed away the inevitable bad ball. Then Waqar played a couple of good shots against Devon Malcolm, and I could see his confidence growing while England began to look ragged and dispirited. All the time I kept telling myself to stay there, trying to calm down my partner, waiting for the loose deliveries. Finally, the winning runs cam as I off-drove Salisbury to the boundary. We raced off to a delirious dressing-room. That was a huge win for us, against the odds, proof that we were getting mentally tougher. To beat England at Lord's, the home of cricket, made it even more special. Only the Melbourne Cricket Ground under lights beat playing a Lord's for me.

Our captain, Javed Miandad, ensured we showed the necessary mental strength throughout this tour, and he was very positive, very astute, and looked after Waqar and I whenever we felt we needed a rest. All of the boys were right behind him but I had misgivings at times about his willingness to mix it with the opposition on the field. Javed has always been one of cricket's streetfighters who would never bow down to anyone, least of all England players, and he came into the 1992 tour ready to take on anyone. Unfortunately that led to a few incidents on the field that did us no favours. There was the odd time when we looked a rabble, challenging the umpire disrespectfully, and that harmed our image. When the ball-tampering allegations broke towards the end of the tour, I'm sure many thought: 'They've behaved badly in this series, I wouldn't put it past them.'

Javed Miandad must take the blame for that because he allowed himself to get carried away, especially in the Manchester Test. On the fourth evening our fast bowler Aqib Javed got into a row with umpire Roy Palmer after he had been warned for intimidatory bowling at Devon Malcolm. Now we all thought that was unfair on Aqib, who had been bounced happily enough by Malcolm in the previous Test at Lord's. Aqib was just as negligible a batsman as Malcolm, and the English players were very pleased to see the bouncers fly around. We made a mental note of that for Old Trafford, and we were all set to give some of it back to Malcolm. But Palmer thought we were overusing the bouncer and shouted, 'Hey! Come on!' in a very rude manner to Aqib.

Now we didn't think much of Roy Palmer. His attitude in county games has appeared superior and here he was, in his first Test as umpire, acting discourteously when we were perfectly entitled to give back to Malcolm some of his own medicine. What happened after that, though, I cannot excuse. I was fielding at gully and had an intimate view of Aqib over-reacting childishly, then Javed intervening stupidly. Aqib started shouting at the umpire, Javed weighed in with his emotive contribution, and it started to get very ugly. When Palmer tossed Aqib's sweater to him at the end of that over, he had trouble dragging it out of his belt, so it looked as if he had thrown it angrily at him. That wasn't the case, as I could clearly see, but Aqib and Javed were still stirred up and the shouting match continued, accompanied by gesticulations and choice language. It was all very reminiscent of Mike Gatting and Shakoor Rana. Then a Pakistani supporter raced on to the pitch, pursued by security officers, and it was looking very nasty. Fortunately, Aqib bowled Malcolm in his next over and that was the end of play for that day. We knew the media would go to town on us, and they did – justifiably so. The match referee fined Aqib half his match fee, warned our team manager Intikhab Alam for telling the press that Palmer had insulted our bowler by throwing his sweater at him, and Miandad was told to ensure his players acted within the spirit of the game.

It was basically Javed Miandad's fault. He ought to have stepped in straight away when he saw that his young excitable bowler was losing his rag at the end of a tiring day. He should have told Aqib to get back to his mark and stop harassing the umpire. There was no doubt that Aqib had been petulant, but it was up to his experienced captain to smooth things out. But that wasn't Javed's style; he looked for confrontation. I underline that Roy Palmer's attitude was unfortunate, but that can't excuse the way he was harangued by our bowler and captain. That regrettable incident was uppermost in my mind when, after taking over the Pakistan captaincy, I told my players not to argue with the umpire, that I would take up their case and that they should get back to the mark. You can't have players surrounding an umpire, squabbling and cursing. We must accept that umpires are the sole judges of play, even though it's sometimes very difficult to grasp for a team that's as temperamental as ours.

We nearly lost it again in the next Test, at Leeds, although I think we had more justification. England needed only ninety-nine to win, but we showed our mettle by coming out like Imran's 'cornered tigers' and grabbing some early wickets. We had a sniff of victory, and when Graham Gooch was clearly run out for thirteen, we were ecstatic. Except Gooch wasn't given out. It was amazing – he was out by three yards, a fact confirmed on endless TV action replays. The umpire Ken Palmer, brother of Roy and an umpire who'd worried us on previous tours. We were flabbergasted and decisions kept going against us. David Gower ws plumb out twice, lbw and caught off bat and pad at short leg, but he survived. The tension was incredible, and we really felt the odds were stacked against us. When Gooch was out for thirty-seven and Alec Stewart followed to make it 65 for 4, we still felt we could do it. One of our team got it right, though, when he shouted: 'Keep fighting, boys – but we'll have to hit the stumps to get them out!' Now I appreciate many sides who come to Pakistan feel the same way about our umpires, but don't forget that we had asked for independent umpires for years to prevent feelings like ours at Leeds.

We lost that Leeds Test because Graham Gooch, England's best player, had been reprieved, and because David Gower batted coolly towards the end. Two of our players were disciplined by the match referee: Rashid Latif for throwing his cap down on the ground, and our wicketkeeper Moin Khan after failing to get the decision when Gower nicked one to him. More trouble, more ammunition for those who were convinced we were a spoiled bunch of cheats. At least we had showed our readiness to fight all the way, though. That might have been a fantastic victory at Leeds if luck had gone our way, because the conditions didn't favour us and Aqib Javed couldn't bowl in the second innings. It was a tribute to Javed's ability to motivate his players, even though at times he went over the top too readily. If Imran had captained us on that tour, we would have been just as motivated, but I'm sure some of our excesses on the field would have been curbed. We did leave ourselves wide open to criticism on occasions, although we were provoked now and then.

It was hard not to be hurt by the innuendos in the tabloids that August. We were being labelled as cheats simply because certain big names in English cricket said so. Neither the ICC or one of their referees, Deryck Murray, had declared us guilty, but I wish they had been more open in their deliberations. So some England players nearing the end of their careers made unsubstantiated allegations, tarnishing a great summer by Pakistan. Not all sections of the English press were so one-eyed, though. The broadsheets were full of praise for the quality of our bowling and our marvellous team spirit. The point was made that the line of attack by Waqar and myself was far preferable to the West Indian method of digging the ball in short, trying to get the batsman to fend off the ball to the close fielders. For years the West Indian fast bowlers had threatened to drive the front-foot shots out of Test cricket by bowling short of a length into the rib cage. We used the bouncer sparingly, as a surprise rather than a stock delivery, and the only intimidation we exerted was on batsmen's toes with those yorkers. Several writers were magnanimous enough to point out that our style of bowling was exciting, that runs flowed from cover drives and on-drives, or that stumps were cartwheeled out of the ground. It all depended on whether we got our line right. At least something seemed to happen when we bowled. And we were responsible for an innovation – two fast bowlers operating a new technique. Since 1992 every Test team has had at least one bowler who uses reverse swing when the time is right.

At the end of that dramatic summer, I was proud at what we had accomplished, but sad that we had got no nearer to an enjoyable relationship with the England players. I had just signed another four-year contract with Lancashire and was well aware that the English game was full of nice people who weren't bad sports. My fond hope was that, some day, we would have a Test series free of unpleasantness between the two countries, with the hatchet firmly buried. I was proud to play some part in that four years later when I captained Pakistan in England. It seemed a long time since Imran's forecast in 1992 that no official Pakistan team would tour England again. I thought that was a little hysterical when he wrote that at the end of our tour, because I knew there had been faults on both sides and we just needed time and space, unlike the tours of 1987 and 1992. Perhaps we ought to have had a hardship bonus though!

CHAPTER 8

The Bed of Nails

WITHIN SIX months of that triumphant tour, I was captain of Pakistan. You might have thought it would have been one of the happiest times of my career. Not at all. Inside a year I was out of the job and, even worse, ostracised by the senior players, condemned for being dictatorial, undermined by my vice-captain Waqar Younis, and barely on speaking terms with anyone else in our team. On top of that, I had to deal with a trumped-up drugs charge while captaining my country in West Indies, a traumatic experience. No wonder I heaved a sigh of relief when losing the captaincy after the players staged a revolt against me. No captain could have stayed in the job in such circumstances.

The underlying tensions to my awful year are important to understand. We were the world champions, we had just beaten England on their home turf, and we were convinced we were about to become the best team in Test and one-day cricket. We became victims of our own complacency, with star players telling themselves they were now big-time, that it was simply a case of turning on the tap for the big occasions. International sport isn't like that, though, and I tried to warn the players against these self-delusions, but there were too many factions, too many on the outside pouring bad advice into the ears of the key figures in the side. Pakistan cricket has often been prone to volatile periods, to cliques of jealousy in pursuit of power – especially the captaincy – and we were about to enter one of those erratic times. It would last for another three years, with the captaincy being passed around leading to a total lack of stability.

The writing was on the wall soon after the end of our England tour, when Javed Miandad was still captain. We played a one-day series in Australia, where we usually do well, but we suffered six defeats in a row against the West Indies, failing to reach the final. We were getting out too cheaply, failing to rally in the field. It was all falling apart, success had gone to our heads. Then came a short tour to New Zealand where we won the Test at Hamilton. New Zealand ought to have beaten us, we were there for the taking, but we bowled them out for ninety-three to win by thirty-three runs. It was just as well that Martin Crowe was injured, otherwise the unthinkable would have happened: defeat by New Zealand, something we have rarely suffered. They batted rashly, Waqar and I took seventeen wickets in the match, and it was all over on the fourth day. I wasn't fooled, though, by the result. We looked at sixes and sevens.

At that stage, in January 1993, I had no designs at all on the Pakistan captaincy. I'd had no experience of leadership, and at the age of twenty-six my sole aim was to carry on taking wickets and scoring runs and be a good team man. On the flight home from New Zealand, Javed Miandad sprung the notion on me. He said he wanted me to be his vice-captain, to groom me to take over from him eventually. I was flattered, but worried, knowing that I lacked any sort of awareness of what the role entailed. In agreeing to his proposal, I was privately hoping that Javed would keep the captaincy for a long time yet, to give me time to learn the ropes. That was rather naive of me – captaining Pakistan has never been associated with any great security, unless the man in charge is Imran Khan. Just a week or so after that conversation with Javed, he fell out with the Pakistan Board of Control and I was the new captain, in the hot seat without any experience at all to fall back on. You don't turn down such an honour, but I was understandably concerned about my prospects, especially as Javed was to stay in the side, despite his row with our administrators. That hardly inspired me, knowing that such an experienced leader was going to be watching me very closely.

My first taste of captaincy was satisfactory enough. We beat Sri

Lanka and Zimbabwe in a one-day tournament at Sharjah, but I didn't read too much into this because both opposition sides were below full strength. Reality hit me straight after Sharjah when we went to South Africa for a triangular one-day tournament that also featured the West Indies. Although we reached the final, we were poor, with West Indies overpowering us four times in a row during the series. They bowled us out for forty-three at Cape Town, and even though the wicket was dreadful, it was a shocking effort. I felt ashamed that we had just made the lowest total in international one-day cricket in front of a large crowd that included a strong presence from the Muslim community. We were all out in just nineteen overs. Something had to be done, so I decided we would have an extra practice session after lunch. We had to get things right, it was time for some hard work and pride. You should spend more time in the nets if you're not playing well.

This decision did not go down well with some of the senior players, and they started to mutter behind my back. As vice-captain, Waqar wasn't helping me, wasn't backing me up. He now had designs on the captaincy as I started to crack up, and some of his friends in the team – particularly Mushtaq, Aamir Sohail, and Aqib Javed – were telling him he should have the job, that I should be sacked. Waqar started to argue with me in front of the players when I desperately needed the public support of my vice-captain. He was too hot-blooded to do that job satisfactorily, too easily swayed by biased advice, unwilling to see that my decisions were for the good of the team. We barely spoke to each other towards the end of that South African tour. I was in a bad way, worrying all the time about how to cope with the defeats, how to get the boys properly motivated, how to avoid losing my temper. There seemed to be no middle way for me. I made a major error when I refused to attend the presentation ceremony after we lost in the final. Someone should have put an arm around my shoulder, told me to put on a brave smile, show I was a good sportsman, and talk to the TV interviewers. Instead I sulked in the dressing-room, desperately low and alone. I was just too young for the job, but I was also lacking guidance and support. My man-management was obviously at fault, but that was due to inexperience. Perhaps I did over-react at Cape Town and was too sharp with the players, but if the captain doesn't take it seriously after his team's been bowled out for forty-three, when does he crack the whip? Of course, I should have cooled down and talked calmly to the players, but I wasn't sure they would have supported me whatever I said. The side was against me, and I was buckling under the responsibility.

It would have been better for my self-respect and prospects of keeping the captaincy if that had been the end of a busy international schedule, but we had to go straight to the West Indies for a one-day series of five games and three Tests. I feared the worst, and I was right. It was a nightmare. Waqar was still my vice-captain and Javed was also part of the squad, and I was feeling uncomfortable about that. Athough we fought back to draw the one-day series, my form was suffering because I had too many other things on my mind. Three of our players – Aamir Sohail, Aqib Javed, and Mushtaq Ahmed – eventually had to go home with injuries, Javed was way below par, and our fielding was very poor. In the one-day international at Trinidad it all fell apart in the field. We went for 122 in the last fifteen overs, I disappeared for six an over, and I had lost control in the field long before the innings was over. I felt that things couldn't get any worse for me. They did.

Just before the first Test we arrived in Grenada for a three-day game. Our hotel was right on the shoreline and a few of us had something to eat while lying on the beach. We were joined by two English ladies and the conversation was pleasant as we unwound after the flight. Suddenly two policemen, dressed in casual clothes, approached us and arrested four of us for possession of marijuana. They said they had found two cigarette butts nearby which contained traces of the drug. We couldn't believe it. We had been on a public beach, it was after nine o'clock on a Sunday, and those butts could have been used by any one of hundreds of people in the vicinity at any stage of the day. None of us had even been smoking cigarettes, but that cut no ice with the police and we were frogmarched to the station. Four of us – Waqar Younis, Aqib Javed, Mushtaq Ahmed, and myself – were kept on a bench for five hours where we were taunted by some policemen and locals, and the press were alerted to the story. So those two policemen got their pictures in the paper, and we were humiliated as we protested our innocence.

We were treated like criminals. I sat there bewildered, wondering what they would say back home – the captain and vice-captain of Pakistan arrested on drugs charges! It was a shattering experience, and we'd have been lost without the help of our manager Khalid Mahmood and coach Mudassar Nazar, the only ones allowed into the police station to see us. Eventually the police got round to interviewing the two English ladies who had been talking to us, and they confirmed no one had smoked a cigarette, never mind a joint of marijuana. At last we were released – without an apology – and the press swarmed all over us. It left a nasty taste in my mouth. The previous year's allegations of cheating in England were bad enough, but now we were being hounded and dragged into a ridiculous drugs charge. It seemed at the time that Pakistani cricketers were marked men.

We nearly came home after that incident. That was certainly the wish of most of our players. The charges weren't finally dropped until just before we were due to leave Grenada, by which time we were in no fit mental state to play the first Test, in Trinidad a few days later. We had a meeting in Trinidad at which Javed Miandad stood up to say we should abort the tour in protest. I dug my heels in, for two reasons: cancellation would harm relations between the West Indies and Pakistan, and I was worried that so many in the cricket world appeared to be ready to get stuck into us. It was time for us to show some diplomacy, especially as we had done nothing wrong. The game of cricket and the millions of genuine supporters in the Caribbean shouldn't be harmed because of the actions of two policemen in Grenada.

I also wondered why Javed was calling for the tour to be cancelled. Since his supportive comments to me on the plane after the New Zealand tour, he had become distant. Clearly he felt I had been promoted too soon, and that he should be captain again. I noticed that he and Ramiz Raja were particularly keen to get the rest of the players to say they wanted to go home, which was odd when you consider that, for some reason, Ramiz and Javed hadn't been speaking to each other all tour! Now they were talking happily to each other, gathering support against my authority. I was grateful to the Pakistan management for backing me up, and I won the day, but I knew that the plotting against me wouldn't end there. I was living on borrowed time.

My neck wasn't going to be saved by improved performances, as we lost the Trinidad Test by 204 runs and the Barbados Test by ten wickets. Our fielding was sloppy, we batted badly, I couldn't find my proper bowling form, and the injuries piled up. In other words, all the ingredients were there for a shambles. We would have probably lost the last Test in Antigua had it not rained, because by that stage we were demoralised. The intrigues were piling up, the team spirit was falling away, and I didn't know how to hold things together. It seems a recurring problem with Pakistan sides over the years. We just don't appear mentally strong enough when rows are tearing the dressing-room apart, and whoever is captain at that time is just lying on a bed of nails, expecting to be put out of his misery at any time. Waqar was no use to me as vice-captain, and I suspected his and Javed's ambitions.

In the Barbados Test Javed lost us the game because of a stupid shot near the end of the third day. He and Asif Mujtaba had put together a battling partnership to get us within sight of the West Indies' lead when Carl Hooper's off-breaks were tried in the final over. With three balls to go Javed hit him for six, a bold gesture in the final over when we just wanted to bat out time, but he got away with it. Hooper put a man back at mid-wicket for the shot Javed had just played, and next ball he tried the same stroke and was caught in that position. It was amazing that such a great player wanted to hit two successive sixes in the last over of the day when occupation of the crease was essential to save the game. I said nothing to Javed afterwards because I knew words would be exchanged that would be regretted later, but that summed up the team's attitude. By then Javed was ignoring me anyway, and soon after the tour ended I had a strong hint about the way that things were moving.

Basit Ali had been one of our few batting successes, playing the fast bowlers with assurance and looking a very good prospect on his first senior tour. I was particularly pleased since I had stuck my neck out for him, insisting he should go to the West Indies. He had made a lot of runs in Pakistan domestic cricket in recent seasons and I believed he deserved his chance. Javed Miandad disagreed, saying he didn't play fast bowling well and that he'd get overwhelmed in the Caribbean. I got my own way, as the tour captain should, and Basit Ali justified my faith in him. Yet when he got home he told the press how much he owed to his mentor, Javed Miandad. I was hurt and shocked. You have to be honest and consistent in these situations. Just because I have little personal respect for Javed Miandad doesn't mean I won't always admit my gratitude to him for giving me my first big break, at Rawalpindi in 1984. I was stunned by Basit Ali's comments. There was no question of my looking for personal glory, but he had clearly switched allegiance to the man he thought would be the next captain. It made sense to him to keep in with Javed Miandad rather than Wasim Akram. That episode sums up the intrigues that periodically go on in Pakistan cricket.

Although I wanted to stay on as Pakistan's captain, I felt helpless at the end of that West Indies tour. My form had suffered badly and I had little authority over the team. Just a few months earlier I had been one of the main men, now I was being frozen out. My vice-captain was barely on speaking terms with me, and I felt our most experienced player was ignoring me. Apart from my coach, Mudassar Nazar, I was alone. The team meetings in the West Indies had been very difficult. I'd begin by talking about our opponents, looking for their weaknesses, and my players would just sit there not listening to me, waiting for the meeting to finish. There were faults on both sides. I was too tense, too ready to show my frustration, not calm enough. When you're one of the main players and you start to lose your effectiveness, that definitely chips away at your authority as captain. The West Indies is a hard place to tour at the best of times, and this had been a poor effort by all of us, with me carrying the can. I'd lost the respect of the players and it was now up to me to improve things before I got the sack. That was in the future, though, for at the time I had never been so glad to see the end of a tour. I flew to England with a great sense of relief, looking forward to playing in a relaxed, happy atmosphere with Lancashire, enjoying a supportive dressing-room again.

Sadly, it wasn't the happiest of seasons at Old Trafford. Once again we fell away in the championship when it looked as if we were going to launch a meaningful charge. It was the same in the Sunday League, and with defeat by Derbyshire in the Benson and Hedges Cup final, we ended up without a trophy. David Hughes, our manager, had to carry the can, and Neil Fairbrother resigned as captain. It was a shame for Neil, but you could see how his form and confidence were suffering in the job. We needed his brilliant batting at its best and it was the correct decision to stand down. After my recent experiences with Pakistan, I could relate easily with how my good friend was feeling. Nobody can step into the captaincy and be a natural straight away; you need experience – as I had found to my cost.

Apart from our under-achievements on the field, I was happy just to be back at Old Trafford. I topped the bowling averages and hit a hundred against Derbyshire in a match that had some dramatic repercussions. That hundred was enjoyable, but it was more important to bowl out Derbyshire on the last day to win the match. I got the ball to reverse swing in ideal conditions, took 6 for 11 in forty-nine balls, and we were delighted to win so comfortably after being up against it! Yet Derbyshire took exception and sent the ball to the TCCB for inspection. The spectre was raised again, and I was being fingered for alleged ball-tampering. The suspicion wouldn't go away. The umpires, Van Holder and George Sharp, had inspected the ball regularly and found nothing wrong with it; in fact they told me how much they had enjoyed seeing such effective swing bowling. It was hot and dry, the wicket was flat, and after fifty overs the ball started to reverse swing and I cleaned up. It was as simple as that.

No action was taken by Lords's, and although Lancashire were exonerated, we were very unhappy at Derbyshire's attitude. As luck would have it we were due to face each other a fortnight later at Lord's in the Benson and Hedges final. So the temperature was inevitably raised, with added spice. That perhaps explains why Chris Adams threatened me at lunchtime. I was walking past his table when he said to me 'You'll know what'll happen to you if you do that again'. I said I'd throw him out of the window if he came anywhere near me. Adams had been buttering his bread roll when he saw me and he still had the table knife in his hand when he stood up and said 'I'll sort you out'. It looked rather hostile because he still had the knife in his hand, but it was quickly nipped in the bud and he was led away downstairs by his Derbyshire teammates. I suppose that must be one of the strangest cricket records of my career – the only player to be threatened with a knife during a final at Lord's! It was no laughing matter though. I was furious – Adams the public schoolboy threatening the Pakistani. Imagine the fuss in England had it been the other way round.

It was such a nonsense, stemming from a misunderstanding during the morning session. I tried to bowl a yorker at Adams, but it turned out to be a low full toss at waist height, and he lost it and ducked into it. The ball struck him on the left shoulder, but low enough for me to think about an lbw appeal. It must have been painful and I apologised straight away. Umpire Barry Meyer thought nothing of it, and nor did I, but Adams obviously believed I was out to get him. He would have been aware that we were all angry our win at Derby had been tainted by their slur, so he must have jumped to the wrong conclusion, that I was out for revenge. By now, though, I had got used to such allegations, and anyway, I would never bowl a beamer at a batsman because it's too dangerous. Whenever I want to frighten someone I bowl them a rapid bouncer, and that's what Adams would have had if I'd been gunning for him. We had never exchanged words before in our careers, so what was his problem?

That dining-room incident was very disturbing to me and my team-mates were absolutely livid on my behalf. There was even more tension between the two sides for the rest of the match, and we badly wanted to hammer them. But they won it fair and square, with Neil Fairbrother running out of partners. I pulled an intercostal muscle during the match and was in agony when I batted, so it ws an unhappy end to an unfortunate day for me. I made a point of congratulating Derbyshire's successful captain Kim Barnett, at the awards ceremony on the balcony afterwards. I assume Chris Adams would have done the same to our skipper if we had won – after all English cricketers educated at public schools know how to behave, don't they?

So it was back to Pakistan and the need to transform my captaincy before it was taken away from me. I was glad our first challenge was to be in Sharjah so that I could get the boys away from the intrigues at home and try to reforge our team spirit, which had been such a factor in our success the year before in England. It was not to be. For the first time since 1989 Pakistan failed to win the trophy, losing in the final to the West Indies. Athougth I missed the final with a broken bone in my wrist, the responsibility was mine. My injury gave Waqar his chance to captain the side, and he led the team in that Sharjah final and the first Test against Zimbabwe in Karachi a week or so later. He was man of the match in Karachi with thirteen wickets, leading us to victory. I suppose he must have hoped to carry on in the job, especially with his associates telling him he was the best candidate, but I was reinstated for the second Test after recovering from my wrist injury. We beat Zimbabwe in a Test they really should have won, but they collapsed from 135 for 1 to 187 all out to lose by fifty-two runs. Waqar and I did the damage, but it would be wrong to assume it was just like old times. If the Zimbabweans had been more experienced in Test cricket they would have pushed us closer and might have won the series. Our batting was brittle and Waqar's brilliant bowling was the major difference between the two sides.

So my first Test victory at the fourth attempt didn't raise my spirits that much. We still had problems in the side. At the end of that Zimbabwean tour we were due to play the final one-day international in Lahore, so, with the series already won, we decided to have a look at a new young fast bowler, Irfan Bhatti. To accommodate him we decided to rest Aqib Javed. Waqar told us he wasn't fit and that Aqib should play instead. He was adamant, even though he had given no indications of fitness problems to me. So we reinstated Aqib Javed. I felt that Waqar had again undermined me. It was a significant gesture, as I found out soon afterwards.

We were due to tour New Zealand early in 1994, so we went off to training camp. I was one of four selectors who chose the tour party, and when Javed Miandad's name wasn't included there was an outcry in the country. Zaheer Abbas, the chairman of selectors, said Javed's form hadn't been good enough for some time and younger players deserved their chance. As captain, I took responsibility for a decision that I thought was correct. At the same time elections were being held in Pakistan and Mrs Benazir Bhutto was elected prime minister. Javed's close associates lobbied Mrs Bhutto to try to get him reinstated for the tour, and although she stayed out of it, the government sacked the board of control and installed new officials. So Javed saw this as another way back into the fold, and he went to the rest of the players in the team hotel in Lahore and they decided to rebel against me as captain. I had already been confimed as captain by the new board, but then they received a letter from the senior players objecting to what they called my 'domineering' captaincy and calling for a new leader. All the top players signed the letter – Mushtaq, Waqar, Ramiz Raja, Salim Malik, Inzamam-ul-Haq, Asif Mujtaba, Rashid Latif, Basit Ali, Aqib Javed, and, of course, Javed. The only player to support me was Ata-ur-Rehman, who played in the same club side with me in Lahore. What really hurt me was that the night before they had all been guests at my home in Lahore. So they were eating my food in my house, then going back to the team hotel to plot against me. They had been my friends for some years, and yet they all turned against me.

I had hoped for a public declaration of support from the newly constituted board, but when they read the letter from the players I could tell they were wavering. If I took the team to New Zealand and we did badly, the board members would get a lot of stick from the public, press, and politicians. Much more sensible to throw the captain overboard and get a new one from the ranks of those rebelling against me. When I saw I had no power base, I said: 'I'll save you the trouble of sacking me, I'll resign.' So it's not true to say I was sacked, I got out in time. If most of the players didn't want to play under me, what was the point of hanging on to the job?

Then the lobbying started. Waqar Younis was convinced he was going to be the new captain. He told the new board that the boys wanted him. His head had been turned by Mushtaq and Aqib, who had started to call him 'skipper'. That was ridiculous. Waqar had shown no signs of captaincy potential and he ought to have concentrated on maintaining his great form as a fast bowler. He was being led astray by his cronies. After a time, when allies keep telling you that you should be the prime minister, you start to fancy it. Waqar had been undisciplined in my time as captain. His time-keeping was poor for a start: he used to keep us all waiting in the team coach just to make a point that he was the star player and therefore above the rules that applied to everyone else. He would stroll into the team room late for a meeting, and it was clear he was challenging my authority. Javed posed a similar problem. I would take them to one side and quietly point out that they should show more discipline and respect for authority. At no stage did I bawl them out in front of the others, yet they said I was too domineering! I ought to have been more authoritarian, singling out the top players for a rollicking in front of the others. That was one of Imran's strong points as captain. He would insist that discipline should spread from the top downwards so that the younger players would be set a good example. I should have been harder on the senior players who wanted a more relaxed atmosphere – no curfews, no fines for being late for practice, no extra nets if we played badly.

It was typical of Pakistan cricket that the politicians got involved in this dispute. Cricket is such a religion in Pakistan that the media coverage is intense, and politicians see the game as a means to power. Whoever gets political power has to reward those who helped them in the elections, so they hand out administrative posts in cricket because they are deemed to be glamorous positions in Pakistan society, with so many television interviews to be done. So cricketers become adept at dealing with politicians and vice versa, which leads to turbulence at various times, with hysteria being whipped up by certain sections of the media. The politicians get a reflected glory if we do well at cricket – especially against India – so the cricket administrators and players get pressurised by politicians. There never seems to be a period of calm in Pakistani cricket, possibly because we are still a young country and the need for role models to inspire the nation is so intense. As a result sportsmen are placed on too high a pedestal, and when we go through a trough of bad luck or poor form, we are swiftly despatched to the rubbish bin and a new set of heroes is demanded. I don't know of a similar situation in any other country that plays Test cricket.

I'm not a political animal at all, and I was hopeless when it came to handling this side of things. The only captain I've known who could transcend all this was Imran Khan. He had the stature, the charisma, the intelligence, the family contacts, and the playing ability to stand above everything. He could hold things together and quieten all the squabbling. If we had produced more cricket captains like Imran Khan – good judges, strong characters, and fine players – then Pakistan would have been much more successful as a cricket nation.

So, as the politicians and media had a field day over my resignation, the new board had a tricky decision to make: should they reinstate Javed and make him captain, or grant Waqar his wish? Fortunately the new chairman of the board, Majid Khan, was a strong man who knew enough about cricket from his own playing days to know when the whip needed to be cracked. He wouldn't fall in with their wishes, so he gave the captaincy to Salim Malik, a fine batsman. Javed Miandad stayed out of the tour party. The board wanted me to go as a player, but I wasn't sure about that. My initial reaction was to stay out of it. What could I say to the rest of the players who had plotted against me? Who would I run to and celebrate with when I took a wicket? They had hurt me by going behind my back instead of addressing these problems to my face.

In the end I was talked around by my new bride, Huma. We had met seven years earlier at a friend's party in London, where Huma was studying psychology at university, and we married in October 1993. We had a wonderful traditional Pakistani wedding which went on for about three weeks. Huma's family hosted an amazing reception in Karachi, and then everyone travelled to my home in Lahore for the 'Valima' reception which celebrates the consummation of the marriage.

I arrived in New Zealand five days after the others, and when I met up with them at last it was a very strained atmosphere. So I kept out of their way and spent the evenings with Huma. She kept drumming into me the importance of playing for my country rather than being its captain, that it was vital I regained my form. I took twenty-five wickets in the three Tests, including two man of the match awards, and it was an odd feeling not to be celebrating with my team-mates whenever I took a wicket. I'd just walk back to my mark and get ready to bowl the next delivery at the new batsman. During team meetings I just sat in the corner, listening intently but saying nothing. If Salim or his vice-captain, Asif Mujtaba, ever asked my opinion on something, I'd answer their question but offer nothing else. Why should I? Other than the occasional 'hello', Waqar and I barely exchanged a word all tour. All I wanted to do was show the cricketing world that I still wanted to play cricket for Pakistan to my high standards, that the captaincy issue wasn't that vital to me any more. Yet the disloyalty of my team-mates, many of them friends, cut deeper inside me, and the best and only way to combat that was to freeze them out and hope that time proved a great healer. We won both the Test and the one-day series, so I was content that my presence as a player had strengthened the squad. And I had a lovely time in the evenings with my wife, with no cricket talk!

I returned to Lancashire in May 1994, glad to put the intrigues and awkward silences behind me. The leg-pulling and the dry humour of the Old Trafford dressing-room was always a tonic for me, but sadly I was only there for two months that summer. We had to report back to training camp in July before Pakistan's tour to Sri Lanka and, understandably, some of Lancashire's members weren't too pleased that I played just six championship games. What could I do? Once I had decided to put the captaincy traumas behind me, I was committed to regaining my status as a top fast bowler. Test cricket was the summit for me and I owed it to my country. It wasn't my fault that we had to go to Sri Lanka during an English summer. The club knew all about this potential clash some time before the start of the 1994 season, yet they encouraged a public debate on the desirability of still having overseas players in county cricket. There was talk about having a season without any overseas player, but although I could understand the disillusionment at Old Trafford, I wasn't sure what good that would do for the English game. Isn't it a plus for English cricketers that they come up against world-class players on a regular basis? Surely that is valuable practical experience? I also think that overseas players give important technical guidance to county colleagues, provided the county has the right sort of overseas player. So I was torn between county and country in 1994, and if it's any consolation to Lancashire members, I lost money as a result. Quite rightly my summer salary was reduced because I played so few games, and I wasn't compensated for that when I reported for duty in Pakistan. So I missed out too!

We won the Test series and the one-dayers in Sri Lanka, and gradually my mental scars started to heal. My form held up, and I certainly preferred Salim Malik to Waqar Younis as captain because he had a far better cricket brain and was less headstrong. Sri Lanka is a beautiful country, a place where I love to play cricket, and with Huma on the trip it was a very enjoyable tour on a personal level. Winning every game was now more vital to me than any lingering captaincy aspirations. I remembered Imran telling me during those traumatic earlier days that you should never go after power, that if you chase too much after something it'll go away from you. That's what happened to Waqar: he made it too obvious he was keen to be captain, even though he wasn't qualified for it. We never sat down to talk through our disputes or our unhappiness with each other, but gradually we inched back to something approaching our previous friendship. It took a couple of years though, but time does take the pain out of things. Both of us realised that it was more important to remain in the team, winning matches for Pakistan. The captaincy issue was just too complex and traumatic – as my successor was about to discover.

CHAPTER 9

Another Fine Mess

IN 1995 Pakistan cricket's image reached rock bottom. For most of the time we were a shambles. We had five captains in that year, and not even England could match that in their darkest times. Salim Malik was accused of offering bribes to Australian players to throw a Test match (a claim later repudiated by an inquiry in Pakistan), and wild accusations about the integrity of all the Pakistani players were bandied around. Two of our players announced their premature retirements, only to make themselves available just a few months later. With indiscipline now common on the field, we were a rabble at times. All of this was powerful ammunition for those who had criticised us in the past for breaches of discipline and allegedly shady dealings. It was the worst time of all to be a Pakistani cricketer. When I was raised again later in the year to the captaincy, improving our dreadful image had to be my first priority. I was under no illusions about my reinstatement. Nobody else was suitable – they'd tried out all the other candidates!

The irony is that the roof fell in just after we had beaten Australia at home in the Test series. Our victory by one wicket in Karachi was our best ever in Tests, in my opinion. Chasing 320 on a turning wicket against Shane Warne was a huge task, and to see our last pair (Inzamam-ul-Haq and Mushtaq Ahmed) add fifty-seven to win the game was emotional and thrilling. We had a lot of luck, particularly with the winning runs. Warne bowled Inzy a huge leg-break that pitched outside leg-stump and beat the keeper,

Ian Healy, outside off-stump. Inzy had overbalanced as he tried to play through mid-wicket, so it was a missed stumping that went for four leg-byes. No wonder Healy was in tears afterwards as our delirious crowd chanted 'God is great'.

That passionate support really hyped us up, gave us strength for what was a fantastic win. The Australians were the best team in the world, a tough unit with some fine bowlers and experienced batsmen, the sort of team that kept its foot on your neck when you were down. That's why it was so exhilarating to win after it looked as if we would fold fifty-odd runs short of our target. For me it was marvellous to line up against such a great bowler as Shane Warne, a genuine matchwinner. I'm sure his presence inspired Waqar and myself to an even higher pitch of commitment: the three of us managed twenty-three dismissals in that Karachi Test as we all battled to take the vital wickets.

We hung on for draws in the next two Tests to take the series, and for this Salim Malik must take a lot of credit. He scored a magnificent 237 and 143 to dig us out of holes, as Warne bowled over after over. Both pitches were dead, which suited us with that precious one-nil lead, and the Australians dropped too many catches. At the end of that series Salim Malik must have felt firmly entrenched as Pakistan's captain, or at least as entrenched as you can be in our side. Within a few weeks he was fighting to maintain his credibility.

Pakistan were involved in a busy schedule as usual, with a three-month tour of South Africa and Zimbabwe to be followed by the Sharjah Trophy in April. Before joining the boys in South Africa for a one-day series, I went to England for a sinus operation. When I rejoined them, just before the final, things seemed fine, but then it all changed dramatically. We were due to play South Africa in a best-of-three final, but we were thrashed two-nil in baffling circumstances. There had already been a few rumours flying around about bribery allegations, and the players were starting to talk. I asked Salim Malik point-blank about the rumours and he told me he knew absolutely nothing about the matter. I persisted and said, 'Come on, we can't just ignore it, what's going on?' and again he denied all knowledge. That was enough for me. I never really believed the allegations about Salim, but the whispers had clearly unsettled our players, and two odd decisions by the captain led to even more chatter in our dressing-room.

Salim won the toss in both one-dayers, at Cape Town and Johannesburg, and each time he didn't follow the conventional pattern of batting first. We knew that local knowledge always recommneded fielding last at these two venues, because the ball boomerangs about later in the day. All the players were asking openly why we were fielding first after winning the toss, and I could only say I didn't know the reason. I was now just another player, not part of the management meetings. So we lost both games badly, and Salim's head was moving towards the executioner's block. Being bowled out for 109 in Johannesburg to lose by 157 runs when you have presented the game on a plate to the opposition by fielding first, that is bound to chip away at a captain's standing in the dressing-room, especially with players wondering openly about your motives. Salim didn't help himself by being such a quiet guy and a poor communicator, so the recipe for divisions was taking shape.

After that second shambolic performance in the one-day final we stayed in Johannesburg, preparing for the Test match. In those few days team spirit and discipline just slipped away. Waqar, who had been taking wickets and bowling very well, was going through one of his haughty phases, talking too much in team meetings and taking no notice of the captain or manager, Intikhab Alam. I felt the new vice-captain, Rashid Latif, was no use at all. To me he was a nice guy, but too keen to fight battles for individuals, trying to be the dressing-room lawyer. He should have just played cricket and supported the captain's decisions, keeping silent about what they said to each other in private. In my time the vice-captains have often undermined the captain and I don't understand why they feel the need to get involved in all the political wheeler-dealings. They shouldn't be plotting, they should leave the captain to carry the can, but offer guidance and advice when asked for it. After all, nobody blames the vice-captain when things go wrong, it should be a job carried out without fuss and back-biting. That's rarely been the case with the Pakistan side, I'm afraid.

During one particular bitter team meeting in Johannesburg, things came to a head. Players were squabbling openly in the room and nobody was listening to the captain. Someone then shouted, 'What's all this about the toss and bets?', a clear reference to Salim's two costly decisions in the recent one-day matches. We all looked at each other and wild accusations started to fly around. I couldn't take any more and I stood up to say, 'This is the worst team meeting I've ever been in, where are the manners?' And I walked out. Others followed me, leaving us in total disarray. Our manager Intikhab realised he had to try to pull things together, otherwise the fall-out would be spectacular and very public. No side goes down the plughole as quickly as Pakistan when we start rowing in the dressing-room, and this was another case in point. Inty produced the Koran and suggested we all swear on it that no one had been involved with betting in any of our matches. To a Muslim the Koran is hugely important, and everyone in that room took the oath.

That volatile team meeting did nothing to improve morale though, as we showed in the Johannesburg Test. That was one of the worst performances I have ever been involved in with Pakistan. We were hammered by 324 runs, and in a masterpiece of under-statement Intikhab called it 'unprofessional'. Salim denied rumours afterwards that there had been unrest in our camp (if only the media had known the full extent of our disenchantment). Our preparation had been hopeless and the team selection amazing in one case. When Waqar Younis declared himself unfit with back trouble, the management declined to select Ata-ur-Rehman, a reli-able fast bowler who was on the tour. Instead they called up a twenty-one-year-old, Amir Nazir, and told him to get over from Pakistan as quickly as he could. Now I had a lot of time for Amir. It was me, after all, who had selected him for the 1993 West Indies tour after Waqar and I had been impressed by his pace in the train-ing camp. He had played in one Test in the Caribbean and suffered no-ball problems, but he was definitely one for the future. He had drifted out of the picture until that summons to Johannesburg two years later, at the shortest possible notice.

After a fourteen-hour flight, Amir arrived at the airport an hour before play was due to begin and got to the ground thirty-five min-utes after the start. As luck would have it we had lost the toss and were in the field, so he had to rush on to the field breathlessly, meeting some team-mates he barely knew. When it was his turn to bowl, he suffered cramp – surprise, surprise. Before the first day was over he had been stricken again with cramp, poor chap. It was ridiculously unfair on him and showed what a nonsense we had become. Nobody from our management had asked my advice on who should replace Waqar, and I was thunderstruck when they announced we wouldn't be playing one of our tour party, instead rushing in a reinforcement from half a world away, then expecting him to bowl in a Test match on the same day.

As we moved on to Zimbabwe it was clear that Salim had lost it as captain in the eyes of most of his players. I recognised the signs, which I had suffered myself only recently: your form starts to dip and you find your players are taking no notice of you when you're trying to make a serious point. It just got worse for Salim. During the Harare Test it emerged that three Australian players – Tim May, Shane Warne, and Mark Waugh – had accused Salim of offering them money to throw the Karachi Test, the gripping game we eventually won by a single wicket. I was astonished. There had been no accusations when they toured Pakistan a few months earlier. Why had it taken so long for the three Aussies to make public their charges? Was there any connection between Karachi and those two one-day games in South Africa, when Salim surprised us all by fielding first? Did the other players know anything? I remembered there had been some talk about betting when I joined them in South Africa after a month away for my sinus operation. What was going on? This thing had to be faced.

My mind went back to a phone call I had received in my hotel room the previous April, in Sharjah. We were due to play India the next day, and the voice said: 'You're going to lose tomorrow.' I asked: 'Who is this?' The simple reply was: 'You know'. That was all. That same evening I got another phone call to say that six Pakistan players has been bought up for the India game. Both callers were male. I contacted Intikhab Alam and he said he'd had similar calls that night. So he called a team meeting. He said: 'We're going to beat India tomorrow, but if anyone knows anything about these calls, say so now.' Nobody, including our captain Salim Malik, could throw any light on these disturbing messages.

We did win comfortably next day, by six wickets, and I thought no more about it. Obviously a couple of cranks. We had got used to some people saying that whenever we lost it was because we had been bribed. It would never be due to the other team playing better than us. I recalled a similar situation in 1990, again in Sharjah, when Javed Miandad was called in his room to be told that the rest of the Pakistan side had been bought up, and that we would lose the next day. Imran Khan called us all together, found out that nobody knew a thing, and we won the following day.

Rumours about bribes have been circulating in Pakistan for some years now because there is such a lot of gambling in our country, and in India. So when you get a surprising result the gamblers who have lost out blame the players and allege there's been a fix. The press shows its gullibility by printing such allegations, and some start to believe in them, even though there's never any concrete proof. Cricket is an obsession to many in Pakistan. We are a young country, and success in world cricket can sometimes be over-emphasised by some who also stake large sums of money on Pakistan victories. Betting is part of the sporting culture on the Indian sub-continent, as much as a few beers are for sports fans in Britain, Australia, or South Africa. You'll never stamp out betting on cricket matches in India or Pakistan.

No one has ever offered me money to lose a match and I know of no occasion when a Pakistan player has either offered a bribe or taken a bribe. I cannot be a hundred per cent certain that it has never happened, all I can say is what I know for certain. I never heard anyone in the Pakistan dressing-room say that Salim Malik was offering bribes, and any comment was only ever about the allegations rather than anything concrete. It would be shocking and sickening to me if I knew of my team-mates had been involved. In a team game like cricket, I would have thought you had to bribe all eleven players, because if you concentrate on just three or four the others will still be trying their best and a defeat wouldn't be certain. It's not like other sports that are individual contests. If all eleven are then bought up, the chances are that somebody else will find out, because it would be hard to keep it a secret among so many.

I just couldn't believe the Australian allegations could be true. When our board of control launched an investigation, appointing a respected judge, Salim was suspended for the duration of the inquiry. The three Australians sent sworn statements to the judge, but refused to travel to Pakistan for cross-questioning. Perhaps they were worried about their physical safety, but their absence didn't strengthen their case. In the end Salim was cleared and reinstated to the Pakistan team, so it's only right that he should be judged innocent, despite the mutterings from Australia. Three years later, when I was accused of being involved in match-fixing, I was so shattered that I had to give up as captain. It was only then that I realised the full extent of the pressure Salim had faced.

Salim had enough on his plate in Harare, apart from the bribery allegations that hit us on the first day of the Test. We were beaten by an innings, and it looked as if things couldn't get any blacker. Salim and Rashid, the captain and vice-captain, weren't getting along at all by now, and we lacked direction in the field as Zimbabwe piled up a big total. I was fielding at fine leg and third man, staying out of all turmoil, just trying my hardest when I bowled. I sent down thirty-nine overs on a flat wicket, but the Flower brothers played me really well. I was getting it to swing both ways, but they blocked the inswinger, played the outswinger according to its length, and just waited for the bad ball. They ground us down over the first two days, then tied up our batsmen outside off-stump, bowling a tight line and frustrating us. We got ourselves out, but to be bowled out in the second innings in just sixty-two overs and to lose inside four days to an inexperienced Test team was another humiliation. I don't feel it was due to the extra pressure stemming from the bribes story, I believe it was just another poor effort from a side whose morale was sinking towards rock bottom, with our captain unable to pull us round because he was besieged from all sides.

We then had another meeting, and at last it was a constructive one. Waqar Younis had gone home with his worrying back injury, so that meant the meeting could be less contentious. We all agreed we shouldn't be losing to the Test newcomers. Intikhab got me involved at last, and I was happy to give my views: we should approach the Tests like the home side, by bowling an off-stump line, waiting for the bad shots, and then looking to score off loose deliveries when we batted. Be patient with bat and ball, get a lot of runs on the board, and then pressurise their batsmen. After that we beat them by eight wickets in Bulawayo and by ninety-nine runs in Harare, so at least we regained some self-respect.

That Bulawayo Test was a bad-tempered affair, with a lot of sledging on both sides, and I was as guilty as anyone. I was really fired up, desperate for us to play with more passion, and for the only time in my international career I was in trouble. In the second innings, after I had an lbw appeal rejected, I snatched my cap from the umpire at the end of the over. It must have looked petulant and the referee, Jackie Hendriks, was right to reprimand me. It was a hot day and to me it was a big 'out', but I was out of order, and I went to the umpires at close of play to apologise. Jackie Hendriks was also called in to look at the state of the ball after the Zimbabweans alleged we had been illegally working on it. This was on the first day, and we thought it was a joke. The marks were caused by the usual wear and tear, not by the need to encourage reverse swing. It was a grassy pitch of uneven bounce, and all we had to do was bowl it in the right area and we'd get wickets. They were bowled out for 174 and then complained. It seemed the normal reaction every time Pakistan bowled out a team cheaply.

It must have been a great tour for a journalist to cover, because there was no shortage of news stories. The final one was the sudden retirement of Basit Ali and Rashid Latif, saying that they no longer enjoyed playing. I had already formed my own views about the character of Basit Ali when he positioned himself in the Javed Miandad camp after the 1993 West Indies tour, and Rashid Latif's decision clearly had a lot to do with his relationship with Salim Malik. They had not been a success, and I think Rashid ought to have been more supportive as vice-captain on this traumatic tour. Their retirement was short-lived: they both came back to play in the Singer Trophy a few months later, in Sharjah. Presumably the absence of Malik convinced them they might enjoy playing cricket again.

We had a new captain and vice-captain for the tournament in Sharjah, but it didn't improve our performances. Salim was sacked as the bribes inquiry proceeded, and our wicketkeeper Moin Khan took over, with Saeed Anwar his deputy. It was getting worse. Moin, a good friend of mine, had no captaincy experience, nor had

Saeed, but I backed them, telling them I was there with advice if they wanted it.

It wasn't the happiest of Sharjah trips for me because the board tried to prevent me bringing along my wife, Huma. Apparently they had decided that wives shouldn't accompany husbands any more on tour, but they never told the players about it. I found out five hours before I was due to fly to Dubai, with Huma already in the air, en route from Manchester. If the board had told me about the new rule a week earlier, I would have abided by it for the good of the team, but I dug my heels in after finding out about it at such short notice. I said I wouldn't go without Huma, and they caved in. It wasn't a case of me being a prima donna and looking for something denied to my colleagues; I felt it was just another example of disrespectful administrative incompetence.

On the field in Sharjah we showed few signs of a revival. With several senior players either injured, suspended or recently retired, we were up against it. Our new captain, Moin Khan, went down with chickenpox, Saeed Anwar took over, and for the first time since 1989 we failed to reach the final. The fact that India won the tournament made it even worse for us. Nothing seemed to be going right and we were in complete turmoil.

Not for the first time, it was a relief to get back to Manchester and enjoy my cricket with Lancashire. I really wanted to do well for them after such an unhappy time away from Old Trafford, and I had my best season, taking eighty-one wickets in the championship and missing just three games early in September when I had to report back for Test duty. Unfortunately, we again missed out on the title when we thought it was within our grasp. On our day we were a match for anyone, and in the middle of August Lancashire were twenty-seven points off the top spot, with a game in hand. Then it went downhill, and we finished a disappointing fourth. We should have won the Sunday League, but lost to Kent in the penultimate game, and they ended up champions. So it was frustrating to end up with just the Benson and Hedges Cup to show for a season of great promise and achievement. I didn't perform all that well in the final, getting some stick from Kent's Aravinda de Silva, who made a brilliant hundred, but once we dismissed him it was a comfortable enough victory.

At least I had played my part in getting us there. Our defeat of Worcestershire in the semi-final was one of our best in my time at the club. We needed 262 off fifty-five overs, and at one time we were 169 for 7 with ninety-three needed at more than eight an over. When I went in, the target was 127 off seventeen overs, but I honestly thought we still had a chance. Two batsmen still to come – Warren Hegg and Gary Yates – were very capable players, and I told my partner, Ian Austin, that we had to aim for around four an over early on. The crucial thing was to stay in, get a sight of the bowling, and look for one big over to get us motoring. When Ian got out, I said to Warren: 'I'll have a go now, but you must stay in.' I hit Neal Radford into the trees over long-on for a big six, we milked Graeme Hick for six an over, and we ran very quickly between the wickets. The rate came down, and when I was out for sixty-four off forty-seven balls, we only needed twenty-four off the last four overs. That was no trouble to Warren and Gary, and we managed it with four balls to spare. The scenes in our dressing-room were so emotional, with our coach David Lloyd in tears of joy. He was proving a terrific guy to lead us. He'd get really involved with his players, backing them all the way. I was very pleased for David that day. He was a great loss to Lancashire when England signed him up the following year.

Five days after my last game of the season for Lancashire, I was playing for Pakistan in a Test match. From a Sunday League game at the Oval to the sweltering heat of Peshawar is quite a culture clash, and I nearly came back to England to see out the rest of Lancashire's fixtures that September. I had taken a twelve-hour flight to Islamabad, hung around at the airport for two hours, then flew to Peshawar. When I got to the team hotel I was dead on my feet. It was the day before the Test and I knew I'd cut it fine, that I had to have a good rest to do myself justice the next day. When I checked in at hotel reception I was told I'd be sharing a room, that the new team management had decided only the captain and vice-captain could have single rooms. For the past five years I had enjoyed the use of a single room, but now the system had changed, at a bad time for me. I wouldn't be able to rest properly if I had to share a room. Why were the players being treated like dirt when we were representing our country?

Our new management team consisted of Majid Khan as manager, Mushtaq Mohammad as coach, and Ramiz Raja as captain. So Moin Khan didn't last long as skipper, and his place had been taken by a nice, well-educated guy who hadn't been playing all that much for Pakistan. I liked Ramiz, but he didn't fulfil the basic qualification for a captain – a good enough player to get in the side automatically. The omens weren't good for players' rights, and when I saw Ramiz in the hotel I told him I'd give him my full support, but he must stand up on our behalf. I could tell he was worried about upsetting the board and I decided to fight my own battles. With my bags still unpacked, I told Majid that I wouldn't stay unless I got my single room; I'd be going back to Lancashire where they treat their players with respect. I got my own way eventually, but it wasn't a great start under the new regime. Just a couple of years after that, I would fall foul of Majid Khan, leaving me out of the Pakistan side.

We won at Peshawar by an innings on the slowest wicket I think I've ever bowled on, so I was pleased to get eight wickets in such humid conditions. We lost the plot after that, losing the next two Tests and the one-day series. Sri Lanka inflicted on us Pakistan's first defeat at home in a Test series since 1981, and it was all very embarrassing. Ramiz showed his lack of captaincy experience by attacking too much in the field. He also couldn't get any runs, which diminished his standing, and Waqar Younis was unfit and overweight, suffering from the after-effects of his back injury. I couldn't bowl after the first innings of the second Test due to a frozen shoulder. I just couldn't move it in the mornings and I had to stand down for the third Test. That was the start of the shoulder problems that led to my awful summer of 1997 when I hardly played for Lancashire. I should have decided to rest it for two months or have an operation, but I kept putting it off, trying to play through it. After a while the pain would go away, only to return a few months later. It wasn't right until the surgeon operated on me in England in July 1997.

My shoulder injury kept me out of October's Sharjah tournament, and again we had a nightmare there. We failed to reach the final and there were more disagreements among senior players, with the vice-captain Aamir Sohail at loggerheads with Ramiz.

Aamir was always an excitable presence, good in small doses, but after a while on tour he would start to manipulate younger players and try to undermine authority. An argumentative character, he was my vice-captain on subsequent tours to Australia and England, but he was never fully in my corner, I felt. It must have been difficult for Ramiz when he was captain for that brief period, knowing he was under pressure through his inexperience as leader, his lack of runs, and the fact that he couldn't be sure of his vice-captain's full support.

Ramiz was sacked after Sharjah, and we had a typical period of blood-letting. The Sharjah management team of Majid and Mushtaq was also sacked, the board of control announced an inquiry into the state of our international cricket on and off the field, and we knew we were a laughing stock on the circuit around the world. On the field we were ill-disciplined and getting ourselves involved in too many flashpoints, and there was no consistency off the field with the captaincy being passed around and senior players taking turns to have rows with officials and team-mates.

In the space of two years Pakistan used six captains, with no real prospect of improvement. Our image had been further tarnished by the bribes allegations and there was obviously the danger that some mud would stick, even if Salim Malik were to be cleared. Compared to all that, the occasional hint of Pakistani ball-tampering was a minor diversion. We were in big trouble. With the World Cup just four months away, we had no chance of retaining the trophy if we carried on like this. Desperate situations require desperate remedies, so they asked me to try to arrest the slide.

CHAPTER 10

Back in the Hot Seat

I CAME back as captain of Pakistan because there were no other credible candidates in October 1995. The board knew it, so did the players. We were in disarray and desperately needed continuity from some area, with the World Cup so close. It was going to be held in India and Pakistan, which would increase the pressure on us to retain the trophy. The idea of going out early from the World Cup in front of our own supporters was unthinkable, almost as unthinkable as those players who had rebelled against me two years earlier now lining up alongside me as the new captain, trying to spark off a revival in our fortunes. But the dust had settled over that dispute, and the experience had made me more tolerant, less intense about the prospect of defeat. As for the players, they probably thought, 'Everyone else had been tried, we may as well give Was another go'!

Before accepting the job, I decided to dig my heels in and try to cement my power base. It had always dismayed me that the Pakistan captaincy had been tossed around indiscriminately, apart from whenever Imran was in charge. There seemed to be no sense of building sensibly for the future, to remove the erratic mood swings from our performances. Having failed as captain first time round, it would have bothered me if I under-achieved again. I was twenty-nine, a mature cricketer, aware of my past mistakes, and I wanted success. The board had to give me some time, though, to prove I had grown into the job. The usual reaction after a series defeat was to sack the captain, and that meant too many senior players kept on tenterhooks, looking over their shoulders, and wondering if they'd be next in line. That had to be one of the reasons why Pakistan lurched from brilliance to abject humiliation in the space of a week. We needed to calm things down, to look at the long-term strategy.

I told the Pakistan Board of Control that I would only take the captaincy if they gave me at least a year in the job. They weren't happy about going out on a limb for me – it was unprecedented in Pakistan cricket. My view was that we were now in an unprecedented situation, so take it or leave it. They said they couldn't put anything in writing, so I asked for their word of honour. I got that, the board announced publicly that I'd be in charge until after the forthcoming World Cup, so I was happy. That meant I'd be taking the side to England, where I knew we had a lot of repair work to do on our image. So, if we failed in the World Cup, I had guarantees that there'd be no over-reaction to sweep me away in yet another round of blood-letting. Considering the hysteria that followed our early elimination from the World Cup, it turned out to be a shrewd move by me to get that guarantee! I wonder, though, if it stored up trouble for me when the match-fixing allegations centred on me in December 1997? I remembered Imran's advice about not chasing after something too desperately, because if the prize doesn't come to you, the disappointment is stronger. So I was quite prepared to insist on that guarantee, happy to do the job for my country but aware that I risked getting slapped down for demanding a measure of security. I reckoned I had about five years left at the top, that enjoyment of the rest of my career was vital, so the captaincy would be on my terms.

One thing hadn't changed though: my appointment wasn't announced until the day after the tour party to Australia was named, so nobody was in charge of the training camp. There was no leadership there, no detailed discussion about the Australians, and yet we played the first Test exactly a fortnight after the squad was announced. I also had no say in the players that were selected. That lack of planning would have to change, but for now it was important to let the players know what my aims were. The Salim Malik affair would obviously be major news on the tour and we had to work out how to handle it. Salim had just been exonerated by the inquiry led by Judge Fakhruddin Ebrahim, so he would be going on the tour. That would undoubtedly cause problems for Salim, especially when he played against any of the three Australians who had accused him of bribery, but to omit him was tantamount to suggesting there was truth in the allegations. He would have to face up to the fuss, and get on with playing. As one of our top batsmen, he was needed, and it was up to the rest of us to encourage him and try to shield him from some of the spotlight's glare.

I told the players that if they were questioned about the bribes scandal, they should refer the matter to myself or Intikhab Alam. The players should insist throughout that they are only prepared to talk about cricket on that tour. I told them we'd be going out to make friends in Australia, a country where we all loved playing. It was time to play the ambassador, time to bury once and for all Pakistan's reputation as stroppy cheats with a shady attitude to betting against our own team. There had been faults on all sides in recent years because we had become embroiled in disputes in every series, and we had to show some maturity and a few smiles. If we were happy, we would perform better. I told the players that I wasn't going to compromise my principles on punctuality and professionalism. The charge against me two years ago was that I had been too dictatorial. Well, I admitted that I had probably handled things too dogmatically, but that there was no substitute for hard work in practice to give us the best chance of winning matches. If anyone was late for the bus, they'd have to find their own way to the ground, then get fined. On the third transgression that player would be sent home. It was made quite clear by me that I'd be looking to the senior players to set the proper professional example. Waqar Younis, who would be on the tour, would have to toe the line. This would be one touring party from Pakistan that would not become an unprofessional rabble. My theme for the Australian tour was to enjoy it, win or lose, but to try our hardest to win.

The tour started badly for us. Within three weeks of our arrival we were two-nil down in the Test series. At Brisbane our fielding was poor and Shane Warne was on top form, and at Hobart we toiled in the freezing cold on a seamer's wicket. So it looked as if we were in for another Pakistani nightmare. Once we got used to the conditions, though, we rallied. Whenever Pakistan tour

Australia, we struggle at the start because of the extra bounce. Our batsmen get undone by the height of the ball – at least ten inches higher – and our bowlers get too excited and bang it in short. It's a case of getting used to the different conditions after the flat wickets back home. That was certainly a contributory factor to getting bowled out for ninety-seven at Brisbane, although I wasn't happy with the lack of application.

Some hard fielding sessions, improved wicketkeeping by Moin Khan, and a resurgence in the form of our spinners helped turn things around. Our young off spinner, Saqlain Mushtaq, looked a real find, but it was the leg spin of Mushtaq Ahmed that delighted the crowds and brought us victory in the Sydney Test. Mushy took eighteen wickets in the last two Tests, and the rivalry between him and Warne brought extra spice to the series. Mushy really turned it on at Sydney and the crowd enjoyed his bubbly personality, his loud appeals, and his cheeky smile. We won by seventy-four runs, and I know that many believed this was because the Aussies had taken their foot off the pedal, having already won the series. I don't think it's in the nature of an Aussie Test player to coast, and they were up for the game at Sydney, no question. It was just a case of Mushy getting his line right on a wicket that turned for him, and not to mention a second-innings blast from Waqar Younis which cleaned up the tail. We had no doubts over the Aussie's commitment, which is what made that victory so satisfying. Mushy continued his excellent form when we crossed over to New Zealand, taking ten wickets in the Christchurch Test, which we won easily.

It proved to be a happy tour. The Australian press were sensible enough about the Salim Malik affair, giving up eventually when they realised we'd be stonewalling all the time, and the public seemed to take to us. I was very pleased that we gave the impression that we'd grown up as individuals, and Mushy's cheerful attitude was a great help to us. Mark Taylor, the Australian captain, was an ideal man to work with in such difficult circumstances. I'm sure he and his players were concerned that Salim had been cleared by an inquiry in Pakistan, but he never showed any disappointment to me. Before the series I had a chat with him and said we just wanted to play good cricket, that we loved Australia. Mark said something along the lines of 'No worries, mate', and he was as good as his word. A good man, Mark Taylor. He was an impressive diplomat when captaining the Australians in Pakistan in 1994, unlike previous Aussie skippers. Mark just got on with the game, playing hard but fairly.

So the burden fell upon Salim Malik in Australia, and it was a difficult time for him. He arrived a week late, hoping the fuss would have died down, but it never went away. He spent long periods in his hotel room, and when he batted, he struggled. Some spectators got after him, and the Aussie players were understandably cool towards him. He also picked up a hand injury in the first Test and clearly his long lay-off during the bribery investigation had affected his timing and confidence. We were criticised for taking Salim to Australia, but he needed time in the middle after being out of the game so long. With the World Cup just around the corner, he was a key batsman and there was no point in leaving him at home, even though that might have been easier for him on a personal level.

I was also criticised in some quarters for mentioning the World Cup in the middle of a Test series, but it was important to have that goal in mind. Of course it was vital to do well in the Tests in Australia, but I wanted the players to build their confidence for the big games ahead. Purists will say that one-day games are a totally different challenge, but it was crucial that my players weren't made to feel downcast at losing the Test series. I'd seen our confidence drain away so rapidly and so often that I needed to keep reminding them of the World Cup. It was going to be a massive challenge to retain the trophy, with expectation so high among our supporters, especially as we were clearly battling against time in our efforts to rebuild team spirit and improve morale.

In the end we failed in our World Cup mission. We didn't get past the quarter-finals, beaten by India at Bangalore, on their home territory. That defeat sparked off some amazing bouts of hysteria back home in Pakistan. One fan committed suicide after firing a hail of bullets into his television set, effigies of me were burnt, and I couldn't go home for three weeks. Our manager, Intikhab Alam, was called before the Senate in Islamabad to account for this stain on our country's reputation. All because we lost a cricket match to India. I took the brunt of the blame because I was not only captain, but I had pulled out of the match against India just an hour earlier. The rumours swirled around: I had been bribed by Indian gamblers not to play, despite being perfectly fit. In fact I had torn an intercostal muscle in my side while batting against New Zealand three days earlier. I couldn't bowl in that match – which was a fairly large clue, I think – and there was no chance of being fit for Bangalore, despite three daily cortisone injections. A torn intercostal is not just hellishly painful, it usually takes a month to clear up. I was finding it hard to breathe properly and sneezing and coughing were awful. And yet we decided to keep this from the public because we didn't want to give the Indian team a psychological boost. That was a big mistake; we should have come clean about the injury so that the public would not get sucked into ridiculous theories about bribes. It's easy now to concede that it was a tactical error, but we were going to play in an Indian city in front of 55,000 fanatical supporters with nobody there rooting for us, so we believed we shouldn't give the opposition extra confidence.

We could easily have won it, but faded away in the run chase to lose by thirty-nine runs. We were ahead of schedule in pursuit of 288 in fifty overs at the start of our innings, with Aamir Sohail and Saeed Anwar really climbing into the bowling, but we lost wickets at crucial stages and we couldn't do it. Waqar Younis took some flak for conceding forty runs off his last two overs, but his critics ought to have remembered how many games he had already won for Pakistan. Our restive fans needed time to calm down, to understand that India had played better than us on the day. We had lost our trophy after the glories of Melbourne in 1992 and our players in Bangalore were shattered about it, but would some of the hysterical supporters get over it?

We were due to fly home to Lahore from Bangalore when we had the first inkling that the mood in our country was dangerous. The Defence Secretary of the Punjab phoned through to say that he couldn't guarantee our safety at Lahore airport, and he suggested we fly on to Karachi instead. Some very influential people had lost a great deal of money after gambling on Pakistan to retain the World Cup, and the players were being blamed, particularly me. So I couldn't go back to my home city because we had lost a match that I hadn't even played in. I think I had suffered more than any of the players in Bangalore; at least they had had the chance to be involved in the game while I sat on, watching helplessly, going through mental agony. That cut no ice with the fanatics who held me responsible for the defeat. My house was stoned, my mother received obscene phone calls, and I had to stay with Huma's family in Karachi until the temperature cooled. When I got to Karachi, I was told I'd need a police escort if I wanted to go out. This was one of the worst moments in my cricketing career. The effect on me was so great that I even considered giving up playing for Pakistan. No one wants to lose, and a few close friends were the only people I felt comfortable with.

Meanwhile, back in Lahore, pamphlets were being thrown at cars stating categorically that I'd taken bribes not to play at Bangalore. One newspaper alleged that I had received ten million dollars to declare myself unfit, while another said that my wife was behind it all, that she held the purse strings and I had to ask her for money. There was no point in suing these papers because they wouldn't have had enough money to pay me when I won the lawsuit, which would take about twenty years to go through the courts in any event. The claims were laughable, but some misguided people believed them, and it made my life very difficult for a time. Sarfraz Nawaz, the former fast bowler, also stoked up trouble. As special adviser to the government sports minister, Sarfraz had a public platform and he used it regularly to denigrate my captaincy abilities and expose the defects of those who had played at Bangalore. He specialised in knocking us and seemed happy to stir things up. I was to experience similar trauma after we failed to win the Sharjah Tournament in December 1997.

Imran told me to lie low, that it would all calm down, but it was hard when your family had been dragged into the abusive and violent affair with your mother worrying about answering the telephone. When I went back to Lahore eventually, I even had to park my car several blocks away from my home in case it was stoned. The lack of respect shown to my parents hurt a great deal. Those obscene phone calls were still coming through for the next two months, and I had to get used to people running up to me, giving me a volley of abuse, and then running away. I went on live television from Karachi and tried to explain exactly what had happened, and although that was well received in Karachi, my name was still being dragged through the mud in my home city.

Obviously the obsession with gambling in the sub-continent had something to do with this hysteria, but I felt that the sustained campaign of abuse against me stemmed from something deeper than just anger at losing out on a bet. It may be that my friendship with Imran Khan had counted against me. Imran was moving into the mainstream of national politics at that time, preparing to take on Prime Minister Bhutto in the next elections, and so I might have been guilty by association in some eyes. So if Imran's political enemies focused on me in the aftermath of that Bangalore defeat, that would harm my friend in the long run. Not being a political animal, I don't know, but it was a shocking experience.

There is no middle ground for the top sportsman in Pakistan; you are either abused for failing to live up to the public's expectations or you are treated like royalty. It's worse before a big game, especially one against India, and can be extremely distressing. People constantly hound me in the streets and there is a great lack of privacy. For a few days people come up to you and say, 'You've got to win,' and then slide away. If you achieve a high standard in your chosen sport you possess god-like status, just as long as you keep up the good work. You never have to queue for anything, it's just a case of ringing up the appropriate official and any paperwork is taken care of in private. There's never any need to book a table in a restaurant, you can just walk in and be assured of the best attention – and you never have to pay. That's even happened to me in New York with taxi drivers of Pakistani background. Back home it's almost impossible to go to the theatre or cinema because you just get mobbed. Now I won't complain about being treated with such reverence because it means that you've achieved something in your career, something that makes your fellow Pakistanis proud, but the downside can be incredibly cruel. There's always a price to pay for celebrity status, and I had to pay it when we went out early from the 1996 World Cup, and again when I just had to resign as captain in January 1998.

I learned one big lesson from Bangalore: if you're injured, tell the public, don't get involved in fruitless mind games with the opposition. We ought to have let slip the news that I was doubtful a day or so earlier to prepare the Pakistan public, and the gamblers, for disappointment. After the game I ought to have called a press conference to reveal the full extent of my injury and try to calm down the fevered reactions back home. If I'd taken the trouble to offer some sporting words to India, to make some diplomatic comments, that could have eased the hysteria, made people realise it was only a game of cricket, not a war for the honour of our country. Instead it was total chaos after the match, and our communication skills were faulty.

Even if I had been fit for Bangalore, we might not have advanced any further because one player doesn't make all that much of a difference. I'd also made a big captaincy error by laying down our strategy of going into the World Cup games with six batsmen. We should have made do with five and picked five specialist bowlers, following on from our successful method in 1992 of using attacking bowlers to get wickets cheaply. On the flat wickets of India and Pakistan, in games that allowed only fifty overs' batting, five batsmen were enough, especially with the back-up of our keeper, Rashid Latif, who was such an accomplished batsman. We were trying to get by with Aamir Sohail and/or Salim Malik as our fifth bowler when the situation was crying out for the specialist skills of our young off spinner Saqlain Mushtaq. He had shown his impressive maturity and variety on the tour to Australia and New Zealand, and he would have been a matchwinner if we had played him more often in the World Cup because he was an unknown quantity.

After we were eliminated in the quarter-finals, I felt sure that Sri Lanka would win the World Cup. There was an element of bias there because I love their country, enjoy playing there, and have some good friends in their team, but there were also sound cricketing reasons for fancying them. They knew how to play on those flat wickets and they had some clever bowlers and a positive game plan under an excellent captain, Arjuna Ranatunga. We ought to have seen their success coming after the way they had beaten us in Pakistan in both the Test and one-day series a few months earlier. In fact Arjuna told me that after winning in Pakistan, he thought Sri Lanka could now beat any side in the world.

They certainly approached the World Cup with huge self-confidence. It was a big advantage to have a settled, experienced batting order, including one of the best players in the world (Aravinda de Silva) and two brilliant openers, Sanath Jayasuriya and Romesh

Kaluwitharana. Everybody started talking about the role of the pinch-hitter in this tournament, to take advantage of the early fifteen overs when only two fielders are allowed outside the circle. No team could touch the Sri Lankans for the way they blazed away right from the start, even when they were 1 for 2 in the first over against India in the semi-final. They were an exhilarating side, and anyone who thought Jayasuriya was just a slogger who got lucky should have seen the orthodox way he batted. What was different was his uninhibited approach. His Test record didn't exactly falter either after the World Cup. Any batsman who can score 340 and 199 in a Test series, as he did against India a year later, is a top player. I believe Sri Lanka's victory in the World Cup was a marvellous advert for a fresh, daring approach, and their open enjoyment at their success was heartwarming. If it wasn't to be Pakistan, then I was delighted it was Sri Lanka.

It was never going to be England. They could only beat the two associate countries, Holland and the United Arab Emirates, in their qualifying group, otherwise they wouldn't have got through to the quarter-finals where they were eventually thrashed by Sri Lanka. We beat them easily by seven wickets, and they continued to look very unimpressive and lacklustre. They clearly had problems within their camp, with Ray Illingworth failing to motivate them as manager, and my Lancashire team-mate Mike Atherton looked very down whenever I saw him. Athers shouldn't have opened in the World Cup, he should have given way to a powerful striker of the ball like Graeme Hick or Phil DeFreitas. He was better off at number four or five, knocking the ball around in the open spaces after the fielding restrictions had been lifted, rotating the strike in favour of the big hitters. It was obvious to outsiders that England were too stereotyped in their thinking. The one-day game had moved on drastically in the previous year or so but England hadn't fully adapted to ideas like the pinch-hitter and bowling slowly on flat wickets, or using reverse swing. They also picked the wrong group of players. Young, aggressive one-day specialists ought to have been out there, players like Mark Ealham, Adam Hollioake, and Alastair Brown. With Pakistan due in the United Kingdom in only two months' time, I just hoped that England would continue to pick the wrong team. They didn't let us down.

CHAPTER 11

Mission Accomplished

THE 1996 tour to England was one of the most satisfying periods of my career. To win the Test series two-nil and to be acknowledged as the superior side by the opposition was enjoyable enough, but in the broader areas of improving our image we succeeded handsomely, and that gave me immense pleasure as captain.

The various spats between Pakistani and English cricketers down the years had saddened me. I had great affection and respect for England, having spent many happy years playing county cricket and living in the Manchester area, so I had no wish to prolong any feuds. The omens were good, with England being captained by my Lancashire colleague Mike Atherton and coached by my old mate from Old Trafford, David Lloyd. One of the funniest men in the game and a passionate supporter of his players, Lloyd could be relied on for a cheery word with us. With those two in charge, the old habit of a few English players looking down their noses at Pakistani players would not be revived.

The signs were also good from our side of the garden wall. After the World Cup, Majid Khan was put in charge of our board of control and that was good news. As well as being an idol as a player to my generation, Majid seemed a good straight guy; you could say things to his face and he would take your views on board. He made sure I was consulted about the players I wanted on the England tour, and I got what I wanted. Our tour manager was also a great choice. Yawar Saeed had occasionally taken Pakistan sides abroad, but business concerns limited his free time. I was delighted he was available for this trip because he had played county cricket, he liked England, and knew the importance of quiet diplomacy. We had a lot of bridges to rebuild, and with a classy guy like Yawar Saeed on hand it wouldn't be quite so difficult. Our coach, Nasim-ul-Ghani, had toured England twice with the Pakistan side and also knew all about the various pitfalls.

· I told everyone when we sat down to discuss the tour that discipline was to be the major concern. Too many English players, their media, and supporters thought we were wildcats and cheats. That had to change. Our reputation in England had to improve for the sake of future Pakistani cricketers. In the leagues, many clubs were preferring to employ Australians, West Indians, and South Africans as their professionals, rather than Pakistanis. Having played in England for a decade, I knew how unpopular we had become. Yet if you give everything on the field and conduct yourself properly at other times, you'll be accepted at any cricket club in England, so I wanted our young players to be able to come to England with their heads held high rather than in the expectation of a slagging off. A huge Pakistani community was there, hoping we would win with style, and we wanted them to be proud of us for the right reasons.

Obviously the press would present a challenge, but I was determined we were going to meet it constructively. The tour would coincide with the publication of Allan Lamb's autobiography, which was apparently so strong in its comments about the Pakistanis that he had to retire. No doubt I would be quizzed on that. There was also the High Court case involving Lamb, Ian Botham, and Imran. My former captain was being sued for libel by Lamb and Botham (a case that went Imran's way eventually), and no doubt some of the evidence would be juicy, with ball-tampering allegations given yet another airing. The press would be looking for any court evidence that would stoke up past animosities between our two countries. My stance on this was clear: no one from our camp would be making any comment. We were happy to talk all day long about the cricket in the coming series, but not about media sideshows like libel actions, which would only help to sell books for Lamb. I was very happy for everyone in the tour party to talk to the media, and we enlisted the support of a young volunteer who worked for the BBC Asian Unit to act as our liaison man, getting the players organised and making sure the media people were happy. We had heard that the Indian tourists had been difficult earlier in the summer, asking for money for interviews, and there would be none of that with us. I wanted our players to be in the limelight, to make the British public realise they were good guys and we were a happy team, enjoying playing in their country. The smile was to replace the scowl; the slate was to be wiped clean.

As soon as we flew in, it felt friendlier. No dogs from the drugs squad sniffing round us this time. There were only three media representatives at the airport, so we weren't met by a barrage of aggressive questions. India were playing in the Lord's Test at the time, the whole sporting country seemed wrapped up in the Euro '96 soccer tournament, so we could ease ourselves gently into the tour without any big fanfare. We approached every match positively, wanting to win every game, and I believe the public enjoyed our attractive batting and varied bowling. The feeling in our camp was that England had flattered to deceive by beating India one-nil, and although David Lloyd was right to keep talking up the credentials of his boys, I believed they would be found out by our bowlers. That's exactly what happened, as they collapsed twice on the final afternoon at Lord's and the Oval. In between, their seamers bowled badly at Headingley on the first day when the pitch was greenish, and then it flattened out, leading to a draw.

We were helped by my winning three important tosses. Not for the choice of innings, but for the choice of ball. We preferred the Reader, England wanted to use the Duke, and each time we tossed for use I called correctly. The Reader goes softer more quickly, and has a tendency to go out of shape, but it does aid reverse swing more than a Duke. It was odd to me that England were so fair about the choice of balls. In any other country the visiting team have to make do with what they're given. The dry wickets at Lord's and the Oval were also ideal for reverse swing, and I pulled David Lloyd's leg about that, telling him he didn't know what sort of wickets would be prepared on home soil. It would never happen in Pakistan! When the West Indian fast bowlers visited us we'd make sure they had to operate on slow, flat pitches that didn't suit their extra bounce. There was no point in giving the tourists an advantage. Yet here we had England preparing wickets that were perfect for our type of attack, helping reverse swing and turning later in the game for Mushtaq's leg spin. Thanks very much chaps!

Despite David Lloyd's brave talk, I think he had too much defeatism in his squad. At the Oval, when I won the toss for choice of balls, Dominic Cork was standing nearby and he banged his bat into the ground in frustration when he heard we'd be using the Reader ball again. That told me we were halfway there already, because we had won the psychological battle before we had even tossed for use of the strip. England didn't seem to realise that they could have used the Reader ball profitably if enough of their bowlers had worked hard on the technique in the nets. You can't just switch on reverse swing, and you have to put extra effort into it when you're out there in the middle. The whole team also has to be disciplined to look after the ball, keeping the rough side dry. There wasn't much chance of that from the England boys; they were too busy looking over their shoulders, worrying about their own places. They were looking instead for the advantage of using the Duke ball and getting demoralised when the toss went against them. That was too negative. I remember getting eighty-one cham-pionship wickets in 1995 when Lancashire used the Duke ball throughout that season. You have to be strong-minded enough to make things happen. England had the wrong mindset.

I'm not sure England picked their best side at any stage during that series. We were happy to face Graeme Hick at Lord's because we've never felt he had the game or temperament for scoring a lot of Test runs. Waqar Younis's inswinging yorkers were too much for him in both innings at Lord's. For the next Test at Leeds, England badly lacked the variety a spinner would have offered once the wicket flattened out after the first day. We were never worried about Alan Mullally, who played in all three Tests. His line of attack seemed just to consist of bowling fast medium just outside off-stump, with the occasional bouncer, and you need a bit more to offer than that on flat tracks. When England dropped Andy Caddick for the Oval Test we were delighted, because we feared him. A tall guy who gets bounce and bowls outswing, he would have been a handful on the bouncy Oval pitch. Instead they went for Chris Lewis, who has never been particularly reliable. On the

Sunday morning of the Oval Test he arrived late because of some trouble with his car. How can you rely on someone like that? Atherton immediately dropped him from the one-day squad that was to be announced that same morning, and I don't blame him. I recall Lewis once missed a Test because he was suffering from a migraine. I couldn't pick a player like that. When you play for your country you go through all sorts of physical ailments. Once, at Faisalabad, I was up all night vomiting and I felt very sorry for myself the next day, but I was out on the field, bowling. You must get used to niggles – and headaches.

Athers needed greater support than he got. Once we got him, we always felt there'd be a clatter of wickets. We admired his tenacity and bravery and were happy that not all of his players approached their responsibilities in the same gutsy manner. At Lord's, after dismissing Athers we whistled through seven wickets for just forty, while at the Oval they lost their last five wickets for only thirty-seven runs. On each occasion we were pressing for victory on the final afternoon, but I remained confident we could wrap it up in time after we had got the captain out. We had the variety of bowling, and both wickets gave something to the bowler prepared to put his back into the job, rather than just wait for something to happen like Mullally. Waqar bowled very rapidly at both Lord's and the Oval when we really needed the breakthroughs, and our relationship was back to normal after a difficult couple of years. I knew he would always answer the captain's call because he is such a proud cricketer.

Mushtaq Ahmed, however, was our most consistent bowler, taking most wickets and proving very economical for a leg spinner, conceding just two and a half runs per over. Even when getting some stick, Mushy wants to bowl all day. He thinks he can get a wicket every ball, and he needs the captain on at him all the time to maintain concentration, but he's a great bowler to have in the side when you're striving to winkle batsmen out on good wickets.

I didn't bowl very well in the series, apart from a sharp spell in the second innings at the Oval. My rhythm wasn't smooth enough and I wasn't mentally tuned into my bowling all the time because I was too worried about making sure the other bowlers were happy; the distractions of captaincy took their toll. Yet my personal satis-

I didn't bat seriously until 1987, when I began to concentrate on becoming an all-rounder. (Empics)

It has been a great boost to have Waqar Younis in the team. We now have a good, supportive relationship on and off the pitch. (Patrick Eagar)

Another highlight in my career was achieving my 300th Test wicket at the Oval in August 1996. (Allsport)

I always enjoy receiving the winner's cheque. In this case the presentation was from Ray Treen after Pakistan had won the 1st Cornhill Test in 1996. (Patrick Eagar)

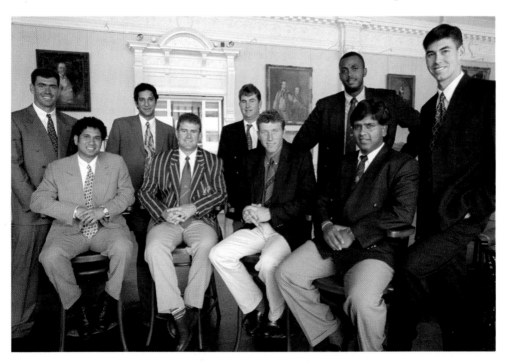

The meeting of the International Test captains gives us all a great opportunity to get to know each other, to discuss any problems and to plan the future of the game. *Back row, left to right:* Hanse Cronje (South Africa); myself (Pakistan); Alistair Campbell (Zimbabwe); Courtney Walsh (West Indies); Stephen Fleming (New Zealand) *Front row, left to right:* Sachin Tendulkar (India); Mark Taylor (Australia); Michael Atherton (England); Arjuna Ranatunga (Sri Lanka). (Graham Morris)

Playing cricket for Lancashire is both a pleasure and a privilege. (Empics)

faction was huge because we played so well, and even England's players admitted we had outclassed them. My one personal highlight came at the Oval when I took my three hundredth wicket in Tests. The last pair was together with Mullally on strike; it was now or never for me, with one wicket left for us to take in the series and my tally on 299. I knew he wouldn't be trying to block me, so I went around the wicket and hit his middle stump with an outswinger. When I saw the ball hit the stumps, I sank down on my knees, raised my arms to the sky, and thanked God. Cricketers take notice of just a certain amount of statistics, and Courtney Walsh was the only current bowler to have reached the 300 mark, so I was proud to have made it. That final wicket meant we weren't going to be held up in our pursuit of victory, so there was relief in my gesture too. We only needed forty-eight to win with enough time to spare.

Our batting pleased me. At last we seemed to have a settled middle order, and Saeed Anwar really blossomed as an opener. I was so happy at his success, because he began his Test career with a 'pair' against the West Indies and after that he was categorised as a one-day player. He tried to blast away like Jayasuriya and was very erratic, despite Imran telling him he had to work hard at his game. There was no room for him in the middle order, so he just had to knuckle down as an opener, without sacrificing his flair. His biggest slice of luck came in his third Test in New Zealand when he made 169. He hadn't been in very long when he survived a confident appeal for a catch behind. It was a big 'out', as he played the ball away from his pads and it took a deflection off the inside edge. The New Zealanders couldn't believe it when Dickie Bird lived up to his 'not out' reputation and reprieved the batsman. So, after scoring just twenty-three runs in four Test innings, Saeed came good with that 169 in 1994 and eventually turned out to be one of the best openers in the world.

Ijaz Ahmed also came good against England after a frustating few years when he was in and out of the side. To me, Ijaz had always been a top player from the time he scored fifty in difficult conditions at Headingley in 1987, yet Imran never seemed to have a great deal of faith in him. He was shuttled up and down the batting order, ending up at number seven sometimes in the one-dayers, and then he was dropped for a time. So Ijaz just had to become harder and more ruthless, and he came back with a vengeance. At one stage he scored five hundreds in five Tests, and he became established as our main man. Like Mushtaq, he's a bubbly character who lifts the side in the field and has what it takes to be a good captain of Pakistan. Ijaz lacks the great natural talent of Inzamam-ul-Haq, but he sets a great example in terms of professionalism.

Inzy was also back to his best against England, particularly with that lovely hundred in the Lord's Test. After the World Cup he lost two stones in weight by working hard in the gym, and it paid off for him. A nice guy, who loves to sleep, Inzy is so talented he can pick up anybody's bat and go out and score runs, but he needs to be chivvied along and told what to do. He lives in Multan, five hours' drive from Lahore, and he usually has no one to train with so he lets himself go at times. I told him to come to Lahore and train with Mushy, Ijaz, Aqib Javed, myself and a few others, and he did exactly what he was told. He worked very hard, sharpened himself up, and looked a terrific player again when he came to England.

If all this sounds as if the England tour was a triumph for Pakistan, that was exactly the case, I can't think of any problems we had (which doesn't sound like a Pakistan tour, I admit!). The rapport with the England players was far better than in 1987 and 1992, and for that I thank Mike Atherton and David Lloyd for their open-mindedness and willingness to come halfway. The younger England players were from the same age group as many of us and we socialised in each other's dressing-room, enjoying some fun times. They didn't complain about being beaten fair and square, nobody mentioned ball-tampering, and the English media were very fair to us, praising our flair. The crowds certainly seemed to enjoy us as well, and we went out of our way to sign as many autographs as possible. The quality of umpiring was up and down, with some dodgy decisions, particularly at Lord's, but we could accept that because it involved a neutral-country umpire. When the umpiring standard dipped, it was the same for both sides, totally above any suspicions of undue favouritism. Take Peter Willey. Some thought he gave batsmen out too readily, but at least he was consistent. David Shepherd was excellent, with a nice, humorous way of dissipating any tension, Steve Bucknor is one of the best in the world, and the Sri Lankan B.C. Cooray was competent. I was also very impressed with the match referee, Peter van der Merwe, an easy-going but firm guy who left you in no doubt what was expected. If the 1992 system had been in place on previous Pakistan tours to England, relationships would definitely have been warmer.

Our discipline remained excellent, and I was really pleased about that because I'd followed Imran's advice about targeting the senior players, and they all responded superbly to the responsibility. For me that tour was a personal triumph, because I achieved all my aims. We'd played successful, attractive cricket, restored a good relationship with England's players, and proved ourselves on a par with Australia as the best side in the world. All priorities on and off the field had been met, including employment prospects of Pakistani players in England. After that tour, Saqlain Mushtaq and Mohammad Akram were taken on by counties, and various league contracts were also offered. So, at last, Pakistan cricket was being viewed with respect in the home of the game, and that made me very happy.

The tour also justified my decision to take up the challenge of captaincy again. After the horrors of 1993 I had grown up and learned how to handle the players more subtly, while ensuring that our standards of professionalism rose. I knew that we were more than a match for any side so long as our eyes stayed fixed on the job, and meeting that challenge was very rewarding for me. Even the press conferences were fun. Having worked hard at getting the right atmosphere and attitude to them, I found them a breeze. It helps if you're winning though, and a smile helps now and then too. Just ask Athers!

CHAPTER 12

What's Wrong with English Cricket?

I'M REALLY grateful to have had the opportunity to play in English county cricket for the past decade. There's no doubt in my mind that the experience has made me a better player, able to perform on varying types of wickets. It has also made me aware that extra fitness is necessary to keep going during the long grind of a season. Pitting myself against other overseas players in county cricket has been good for my pride in my performance; I wanted Lancashire to feel that, overall, they were getting good value out of me. I've had such fun with the Lancashire boys that I'll always look back on my time at Old Trafford with great affection and satisfaction.

There is so much to admire about English cricket: the administrative efficiency at county club level, the facilities, the knowledgeable spectactors, and the generally high standard of umpiring. All of that came home to me very quickly in my first season in 1988. So I don't want my criticisms of the state of English cricket to sound like negative knocking. It's simply a case of being concerned for the future and being aware of the need to get the structure right.

Having a go at the presence of overseas players is irrelevant. You're now only talking about one player on the staff rather than the situation as it was about twenty years ago when some counties had as many as four on their books. That did nothing for the development of promising young English players, but now, with just one per county, there's plenty of scope. The overseas fast bowler won't be bowling all day, and the top batsman doesn't face every ball in his county's innings, so it's a red herring to assume that the inclusion of a non-native player is holding back the development of the English cricketer. It's up to the county to choose the right overseas player, someone who will provide technical guidance and mental advice as well as perform on the field with spirit and pride. Then you hope to get lucky. Lancashire supporters were understandably dismayed when they lost my services for the best part of the 1997 season due to my shoulder injury, but they can't have felt as bad about it as me. I don't see how my absence weakened the case for having an overseas player, it was just bad luck. More and more influential voices in English cricket have started to discuss the advisability of doing away with overseas players in county cricket, but banning us will do no good. There are still ten other places in each county side to be filled, ample opportunity for an ambitious young player who dreams of playing for his country one day.

During the 1997 season, the country had endless debates about the direction of English cricket and the measures needed to improve the performances of the national side. The report from Lord McLaurin, the chairman of the English Cricket Board, was eagerly awaited, but when it came it was an anti-climax. That wasn't the fault of Lord McLaurin, it was more a reflection on the fact that selfish parochial interests had beaten his proposals for reform. For me, two divisions would have been a shot in the arm, bringing the extra pressures of promotion and relegation to sharpen up the playing approach. Now I realise that Lancashire's championship performances in 1997 might have led to relegation, but that would have been our fault, and such a threat would certainly have toughened up our competitive attitude. Instead, the counties near the bottom of the championship table scuppered Lord McLaurin's plans, and an extra one-day competition was grafted on to the domestic programme. That is madness. The players in England have said it so often that it's like a broken record: they play too much cricket.

I believe the talent is there to improve the England national side, but they need help with the structure. Play less cricket, and make it more competitive. So often I hear county players say, 'Oh God, we've got another game tomorrow', and that negative thinking shows in the quality of cricket. I was surprised and pleased that the England selectors took a chance on Ben Hollioake against the Australians because usually talented young players are held back by England until they've proved themselves in the daily grind of county cricket. By then the spark has gone, they've been worn down.

Glenn Chapple, my team-mate at Lancashire, is a case in point. After bowling fast and well on the 'A' tour to India, he should have been fast-tracked into the senior side straight away; instead he bowled too much for Lancashire, picked up a few injuries, and now he's a long way off contention. Yet Glenn has the ability to play for England. Matt Maynard, Glamorgan's captain, ought to have been given the same chances as Graeme Hick for England, but he was in and out. The way Maynard walks to the wicket shows he means business, that he won't be intimidated, but England didn't show enough faith in him. Ally Brown is another. He's the perfect one-day batsman, yet he didn't play against Pakistan in 1996, despite smashing a hundred against India earlier that summer. He gets sent back to Surrey, is told to score more runs consistently, and loses his momentum. County cricket isn't the true test of a player's ability to withstand pressure at the highest level. It's an aggressive attitude that counts, an awareness that a certain player feels he belongs on that stage. Maynard has it, Hick doesn't, in my view. Playing too much cricket leads to jaded players who can't raise their game. Get them in when they're teenagers, like we do in Pakistan, when they have no fear. Would England have selected Sachin Tendulkar when he was just sixteen, or would they have insisted he learned his trade first on the county circuit?

English fans keep asking me why their country turns out no fast bowlers and my answer is always the same: because they play too much cricket and they're shattered halfway through the season. In Australia, South Africa, and Pakistan, about twelve first-class games a season are played so that for every game the players are fresh and highly motivated. Every player should look forward to each game rather than operate on auto-pilot, yet an English fast bowler has to look for quantity – churning out the overs – rather than quality. They are too tired to work on new techniques in the nets, so learning something like reverse swing is too much for many of them. When they get promoted through the ranks they come up against class batsmen on flat Test wickets, and they've got little to offer. You can get by sometimes if you have raw speed, but you still need to adapt to think out the best players. If you're too tired or injured you can't learn your trade in the nets, you just go through the motions, testing out the various niggles. More detailed practice is needed, and less time out in the middle.

The quality of bowling is England's problem, and has been since the days of Ian Botham and Bob Willis. I believe England have some high-quality batsmen – Graham Thorpe is very good, Mike Atherton secure, and Alec Stewart has always been aggressive and authoritative – but that won't help them win Test matches. I look at bowlers like Phil DeFreitas and Chris Lewis and wonder at their continued selections over the years. Lewis has never appeared to have the drive or the grit to go through a brick wall for England. The talent is there – he's been one of the few English bowlers to take to reverse swing – but too often he either pulls out with an injury or fails to deliver when the chips are down. I played several seasons at Lancashire with DeFreitas, and although I got on well with him, I felt he lacked commitment. A natural athlete, he never seemed to do any training but he was always fit, so he ought to have used that time to develop his bowling skills, but he didn't seem to want to know. Phil was stubborn, and when criticised he'd get down on himself and brood. He wasn't open-minded enough to be a successful international player, yet England kept playing him, even when Mike Atherton was captain. I knew Athers didn't have a great deal of time for Phil, so why did he keep giving him another chance? He's never really discovered the consistency and mental strength to go with his natural talent, yet he's played more than a hundred one-day internationals and over forty Tests.

In Pakistan, we're not bothered about our leading players appearing in domestic cricket. That should be the case for the elite in the England squad. You need to keep your squad together as much as possible, rather than see them drift off to their counties. I can't imagine what it does for the morale of an England player to hear he's been dropped for the next Test, then he's got to go out and perform for his county that same day. The day will soon be coming when the English Cricket Board will have these players under its contract, rather than the county's, so the players will turn out for their counties when they're fresh and ready to give of their best, rather than drag themselves up and down the motorway after playing for England and then be expected to shine the following morning.

Take Mike Atherton, for example. On the final day of the Lord's Test of 1997 against Australia, he batted hours to help stave off defeat, and he was shattered afterwards. Having seen Mike at close quarters many times, I know how much such a brave effort would have taken out of him. Yet the following morning he was on parade at Old Trafford playing in a NatWest Trophy game – against Berkshire! No offence to Berkshire, but it was ridiculous to expect the England captain to play against them after helping to save the Ashes Test, on top of all the other demands over those five days at Lord's. No wonder Athers sleeps a lot in the dressing-room when he comes back after a Test. He was right not to become Lancashire captain when he got the England job, because that would have meant far too much on his plate: having to attend committee meetings, keeping an eye on players, sorting out selections. As it is now, he comes back from England duty mentally shattered and plays loosely. So Lancashire have one of their best batsmen playing below par most of the time. Mike was very impressed when I told him how Pakistan unwind after a Test match at home. We spend three or four days together having a debriefing, practising every day, working on our skills, and staying in the same hotel. The idea is to foster team spirit and focus on what went on in the Test that's just finished. Honing our techniques is an important part of those sessions. You need to be curious to see what is possible, especially when you're a bowler.

Athers has taken a lot of stick since he became captain of England in 1993, but I don't see why he should be blamed for too much. Over the past decade England have chopped and changed captains, appointed different chairmen and coaches, and yet they still fail to impress, still can't achieve consistency. So the logical explanation is that the system is wrong. Mike has been the only sensible option as captain because he's worth his place in the side and has earned respect by the professional example he has set. Nobody is a born leader, as I know from bitter experience, and you have to gain knowledge. It did Mike no favours when he was hailed as a future England captain as soon as he came to Lancashire from Cambridge University. That meant he couldn't come to the job in his own time, after observing at close quarters how it should be done. He was thrown into it at the age of twenty-five against the world's best side, Australia, and he just had to sink or swim.

I believe Athers has improved as England captain, and I'm sure the support of his former county coach David Lloyd has been valuable. When I captained Lancashire for a few games in 1995, David was a tremendous help: he only wanted the best for the players, he was totally supportive, and he never forced his views on me, but he was always there for advice. Until David joined England I was never sure how much support Mike got from the likes of Ray Illingworth and some of the other selectors. Mike's still a shy person. He's basically the same bloke he was ten years ago: straightforward, quiet, not a show pony who talks about himself, but warm-hearted. I think his shyness has affected his leadership skills though. Sometimes you have to put on a brave face in front of the team, but Athers lets the mask slip at times and shows his exasperation. He needs to show his authority more on the field, to let the batsmen know he's after them. At times, when the batsmen are on top, the game appears to be drifting, and Athers ought to communicate more with his team and induce some aggression, like the Australians or the South Africans. I appreciate that may be difficult when you're short of bowling class, but you must appear to be expecting a wicket the very next ball.

Mike can also be very stubborn, and at times that veers towards obstinacy. In 1997 we talked about Phil Tufnell. I told him that I rated him highly, that all he needed was firm handling, and that he should be in the England side ahead of Robert Croft. Athers wouldn't have it; Croft was the superior bowler and was also more reliable. I kept on at Mike whenever I saw him, and finally Croft was dropped. Tufnell came in for the last Test against the Australians at the Oval, he took eleven wickets to win the game, and Athers decided to stay on as captain after that encouraging victory. I don't believe Croft would have bowled so well or been such a matchwinner, so there's a case for saying Phil Tufnell prolonged Mike's captaincy career. Yet Mike had backed Croft all summer until the Oval, despite the obvious evidence that the Aussies were very comfortable against him. It's good that the captain shows loyalty to his players, but you must be more open-minded in the face of hard facts.

All the talk about the England captaincy obscures the real issue: that the class players aren't coming through in great numbers because of the system. Since they beat Pakistan in 1982, England have lost to us in five successive Test series, winning only once in those nineteen Tests, so it's not a case of success coming in cycles, as some traditional English diehards keep claiming. The national attitude has been too insular. England's players love touring Australia, New Zealand, and South Africa because they feel comfortable there, but they don't seem to understand that the gospel of cricket has been spread far and wide. Pakistan's senior players have been to Toronto, Singapore, and Kenya in recent years, while England moaned throughout their time in Zimbabwe because things weren't to their satisfaction. What did they expect? Things are never quite as good as when you're playing at home, but you must try to overcome the hassles. The Pakistan Board of Control is very keen for us to play in other parts of the world so that the game isn't confined to just a few countries. The Toronto tournament in 1996 and the following year were two of the best-organised competitions I have been involved in. The matches were beamed live by satellite to an audience of more than two hundred million in Asia, South Africa, Canada, and the USA. It was such a success that Sri Lanka, the holders of the World Cup, have agreed to take part in the next tournament. No sign of England getting involved though.

Sharjah is an even better example of England's negligence. After a gap of ten years, they finally sent a team out for the tournament in December 1997, but they ought to have been out there every year. The Sharjah one-day tournaments have been a terrific education for many top players from India, Pakistan, and Sri Lanka in particular. They were the brainchild of an Arab businessman, Mr Abdulrahman Bukhatir, who studied in Pakistan but wanted to build a cricket stadium in the Arabian desert. He ploughed two million pounds into the project, and in 1985 a brand-new stadium was opened just outside Sharjah. They were ahead of their time out there, using third-country umpires long before the ICC saw sense.

The cricket in Sharjah is very competitive, as you'd expect in a country where around 700,000 Indians and Pakistanis have come to work. It's a great experience, and the matches are designated official one-day internationals. I appreciate the April tournament would be difficult, with the county season about to start, but the October competition should be ideal for England. They would have had time to recuperate after the county season ended a month earlier. There are only a handful of games spread over ten days, so there's no time to get jaded.

There's no doubt that playing on the slow, low pitches in Sharjah have helped many of us learn how to bowl with variety and brains. I went there within a few months of my international debut, and Waqar Younis had his first Pakistan tour out there, and I'm convinced that our ability to bowl reverse swing was honed in the dry, hot conditions of Sharjah. This is one of the reasons why England have been overtaken by other sides in one-day cricket, the competition they in fact started in the early sixties. When Zimbabwe beat England three-nil in the one-day series at the start of 1997, all the talk was about how badly England had played. Nobody seemed to give credit to Zimbabwe, a young country in cricket terms who had embarked on a crash course of education that included trips to Sharjah. Sri Lanka came from nowhere in English eyes to win the 1996 World Cup, but not if you'd seen them play out in the desert, year after year. No Pakistani cricketer was surprised.

The sooner England realise they have to spread their wings, the better for them. I know that the MCC has been a brilliant ambassador for cricket all over the world, but I'm talking about getting the top players familiarised with different conditions. A little humility wouldn't do any harm either. The World Cup has been won by an Asian country in three out of the last four tournaments, and the balance of power is moving away from England and Australia, the old administrative rulers of worldwide cricket. England haven't toured Pakistan for a Test series since 1987. They are due in the year 2000 but they shouldn't delude themselves that our cricket fans are as desperate to see them as the South Africans were in 1995, when England went there for the first time in thirty years. In Pakistan the big draws are India and Sri Lanka, followed by the West Indies. England and Australia are both down the list, although at least Australia do come for a tour every now and then. England give the impression that they'd be doing us a big favour by touring again, but that's not so. I know that many of the current England players are becoming more tolerant and would probably enjoy a Pakistan tour, but we're not that worried about such a long gap. In our experience, their players have moaned too much in our country – and besides, we'd like some stiffer competition!

I do feel sorry for the England players and the amount of cricket they face each season, but that's as far as it goes. English pros complain too much about little things and I don't understand why. At Old Trafford everything is laid on for the players, but I still hear them having a moan about trivial matters. Perhaps that's due to tiredness, but I do smile to myself when I hear some of my Lancashire team-mates say they're looking forward to a holiday at the end of the season, and that they don't plan to do much for a few months. Our board of control's attitude is that you can have a holiday when you've retired, but for now you must practice. After my summer at Old Trafford, or after I've been on a tour, I go home and play or practice every day. Every day. I'm a twelve-months-a-year cricketer, and that applies to the other senior Pakistan players. Since becoming an established player in the national side in 1985, I have had two holidays, to the Maldives and Paris, both for less than a week, both with my wife. Our attitude is that playing cricket and training *is* a holiday.

Back home in Lahore, I leave my cricket bag in the boot of my car and go to one of the ten clubs that are in my vicinity every day. It may just be a few hours' light training, I might go a week without picking up a bat or ball, but I'm still putting in work daily that will help prolong my career and improve my skills. Imran started that trend, and the younger players followed the lead of a great cricketer who still had enough self-discipline to train every day. He was also very strong on the dangers of alcohol, warning us that it would disturb sleep patterns and leave us dehydrated the next day in the field. So that helped us concentrate on our fitness. In contrast many English cricketers spend too much time propping up a bar, breathing in cigarette fumes, and standing up for long periods when they ought to be resting their legs. Their social culture is different to ours, and I understand that cricket in England is closely associated with having a good time afterwards in the bar, but it doesn't help a top player maintain high standards of fitness.

England players, in addition, don't realise just how well they are now paid. For a home Test, the basic is now about £3,000 with all sorts of other bonuses kicking in. The captain gets more than £4,000, and that's very good work for a week. There's also a nice sponsored car for the England player, so the young ambitious guys on the county circuit can't complain about a lack of financial incentives to work hard. I'm well aware that wages for top English footballers are now astronomical and that their counterparts in cricket are envious, but that's just a fact of commercial life. David Beckham at one Old Trafford will earn substantially more than Mike Atherton at the other Old Trafford because football is the national sport, a worldwide game with huge backing from television, whereas cricket is only important in certain parts of the world. It carries little weight in the Far East or the Americas at the moment, so it's unrealistic to compare cricket with football in terms of financial benefits.

What I will say is that the top English cricketers are far better off than the Pakistanis. Our match fees are about £350 for a one-day international and £500 for a Test match, and our daily allowance on tour is fifty dollars – that's around twenty pounds. Unlike Mike Atherton, I get nothing extra for being captain. I've had a number of good advertising contracts in Pakistan with Pepsi-Cola and other products, but that stems from achieving something on the field. As soon as I stop delivering the goods out in the middle, those contracts will dry up. So I have been very grateful to Lancashire for their generous support over the years, and my $35,000 benefit from Sharjah was also most welcome. You don't become mega-rich playing for Pakistan, and I am amused when I hear young English cricketers moaning about their salary and the quality of their sponsored car. It's different again in India, a country of nine hundred million compared to the one hundred and fifty million living in Pakistan. All the major multinational companies operate in India, and the market for a successful sportsman is huge. Someone like Sachin Tendulkar is mega-rich due to so many endorsements. In comparison to India, the Pakistan cricketer needs to keep working hard to sustain a comfortable lifestyle.

The amount of cricket we play around the world may appear tiring, but I certainly enjoy it. At least we don't suffer from the concentrated amount that affects English players so much in their summer. Yet I have the feeling that if the English summer programme were slimmed down, and more tours were organised for the top players, their skills would flourish. Sometimes they do nothing for up to three months in an English winter, and I believe that is wasted time. You learn from playing – in all conditions around the world. That's one of the reasons why the worldwide game has passed England by.

CHAPTER 13

Great Players of My Time

YOU DON'T always appreciate the quality of an opponent in the heat of the moment. You're too pumped up, trying your best for your own side, and don't welcome the opportunity to admire the batsman you're trying to prise out, or the bowler who's running through your batting. It's only afterwards that grudging respect turns into genuine admiration. Looking back on the great players I've played with and against, I'm only grateful that at times I've been able to compete with them on level terms.

IMRAN KHAN was both a great captain and a world-class player. He was the best captain I played under for a combination of reasons: tactical awareness, a positive attitude, inspirational leadership that dragged matchwinning performances out of key players, and expertise as an all-rounder. He could be very stern to batsmen who lost their wickets at difficult times. You'd dread making your way back to the dressing-room, knowing Imran would be waiting for you, demanding 'What the hell was that?' in front of the rest of the squad. If you got out slogging, that meant you were scared in Imran's eyes, and fear was something he would not tolerate.

He used to say, 'Look at Wasim, he's much more talented than me,' and he believed it. To those who just saw Imran as aloof and egotistical, he was surprisingly modest about his bowling. He had to change his action in the mid-seventies to avoid being a bowler who just bowled inswingers, and his subsequent success was due to hard work. I believe that Waqar Younis and myself are probably more talented fast bowlers than Imran because we have more variety and pace. You hardly saw Imran manage to bowl outswing with the new ball; he'd rely instead on the inswinger or the leg-cutter, wrapping his fingers around the ball, giving it a big enough rip to make it go away from the right-hander. He kept going though – a great tribute to his standards of fitness and proud professionalism. His batting just got better and better in his late thirties. Imran was an authentic number four or five batsman, irrespective of the fact that his tally of 362 Test wickets has only been surpassed by four other bowlers.

Captaincy made him an even better batsman, because he then led by example, but the key to his eminence as a batsman was his mental strength. He was so proud, so determined. Waqar and I learned so much from him, especially that desire to win, that conviction we could beat any side in the world. Imran's stature was so massive that it would have been unthinkable to see his captaincy taken from him, and that is some statement when you consider the dramas we've had in Pakistan cricket. He was the only captain who took the job whenever he wanted it, sitting out some series because he felt the opposition was too weak or the tour didn't appeal. No one else would get away with that, but he deserved to.

MARTIN CROWE was the best player of reverse wing I've ever seen. The New Zealander was a model of technical correctness at all times and a formidable proposition on all wickets, but he had the extra dimension of working out the best method against particular styles of bowling. His technique against reverse swing was to play for the inswing with a straight bat. If the ball turned out to be an outswinger, it would miss the bat and stumps as long as he steeled himself not to chase it. Crowe would play forward, with bat and pad together, and he'd be happy to block us for hour after hour. If you bowled him a bouncer, he'd just duck under it, and you'd end up wasting energy. Crowe was such a masterful player that he'd set himself to get runs at the other end, easing into positive mode, and then blunt either Waqar or myself for the next over. It takes a special batsman to be able to do that, without appearing frenetic or stolid.

At Lahore in 1990 he batted magnificently in a losing cause, with

Waqar bowling brilliantly. He ended up 108 not out, made in more than nine hours, and it was a masterpiece of controlled discipline. Not even Waqar at his best could dislodge Crowe, and the duel between these two proud cricketers in that series was stirring stuff. Waqar got him twice in six innings, but Crowe paid him the great honour of saying it was the most sustained quality of fast bowling over a series he had faced. You treasure a compliment like that from a player like Martin Crowe. He knew all about batsmanship.

BRIAN LARA is a different player to Crowe. The New Zealander could just shut you out when everything was right for him at the crease, whereas with Lara there's always the chance that his natural, easy brilliance might be his undoing. Lara seems to have so many options available, and his eyesight is so sharp, that there are times when it's impossible to contain him. I've never known a batsman find the gaps in the field so regularly. That's because he plays so late, so he can toy with the fielders, easing the ball between them at the very last instant with amazing adjustment.

I first bowled at him during the World Cup of 1992, at Melbourne. He retired on eighty-eight not out, courtesy of a bang on the toe from one of my yorkers, but not before he hit the best shot that's ever been played against me. I dropped one fractionally short of a length in the area where a good player would nudge me off his hips for a single. Lara didn't bother with that; he jumped into the ball, and with both feet off the ground he swivelled into a pull shot that rifled the ball to the square leg boundary. It was a remarkable stroke, one which soon became his trademark, the shot of someone with electric reflexes. Now I've never been the kind of bowler to let a batsman think I've been rattled, but as I walked back to my mark, I thought: 'This guy can bat.'

A year later, he hammered us whenever we came up against him. Reverse swing didn't seem to trouble Lara, his eyesight was so good he saw it clearly through the air and knew where he should be playing. With that huge backlift, it was a surprise he was rarely bowled by reverse swing. You'd think he'd be a candidate for the yorker, but he'd just wait to go with the late swing and ease into the gaps. Only boredom and commercial distractions will prevent him piling up the records. Lara can humiliate bowlers who are fully entitled to believe they are bowling well at him, but then you look up at the scoreboard and are amazed at how quickly he scores his runs.

ARAVINDA DE SILVA doesn't get Lara's glamourous headlines in England or the Caribbean, but I rate him so highly. Apart from Martin Crowe, I've had more problems bowling at this guy than anyone. No batsman has hit me so often and so easily. Aravinda's not a copybook player, but he takes you apart with strokes you're just not expecting. He's the one player who can hook or pull the good-length delivery, leaving the bowler demoralised. With a magnificent eye, he can murder you, and he never seems out of form, even though he's now in his thirties. Pitch the ball up and he'll drive you anywhere, bowl him the bouncer and he'll ignore the hook shot, drop one short and he'll cut you savagely. Aravinda gets runs at speed. When he smashed 127 off just 156 balls against us in the Colombo Test of 1994, he went to his hundred with a six, a rare enough feat in Test cricket. Not for Aravinda: this was his seventh Test hundred, and the third time he'd raised three figures with a six. And since then, he's got even better.

It can be tiring being an overseas player who turns out in so much international cricket for the rest of the year, but a spell in English conditions improves your game. Aravinda's year with Kent was very valuable. You're bound to improve as a batsman, playing so many innings, and he tightened up his defence without sacrificing flair. Now he likes to stay at the crease for hours, and that spells trouble for the bowlers. In the Benson and Hedges Cup final in 1995 he played one of the greatest one-day innings I've ever seen. When Aravinda walked in to bat, Ian Austin was bowling very well, a tight line with swing. I said to him: 'Whatever you do, don't give him one short of a length, because he'll be on it like a shot. Give him a full ball.' My thinking was that he might be vulnerable early on to an lbw shout or a catch behind as he shuffled across to a good-length delivery. Ian did exactly the right thing – and the ball was flicked off Aravinda's legs into the Mound Stand for six. The same happened soon afterwards. The bowler couldn't be faulted, it was just brilliant batting.

Aravinda made 112 off ninety-five balls and he almost took the game away from us, until he holed out in the deep. There was no slogging, it was pure quality of the highest class. He played every shot against me – the pull, the cut, the drive, and the straight push past me to the slower delivery. I didn't know where to bowl at him, although I never backed down, believing that the best form of defence is attack. That did me no good though – it was Aravinda's day and he gave fantastic entertainment that was fully appreciated by the Lancashire supporters as well. Not many players get the Gold Award when they've been in the losing side at Lord's, but that day there was only one candidate.

SHANE WARNE is a captain's dream. Not only does he take wickets, they don't cost much. For a leg spinner to concede just two and a half runs per over while turning the ball so sharply is vary rare, and Allan Border and Mark Taylor owe a great deal to this man for their successful periods as Australia's captain. When you've got a bowler like Warne in your side, the game looks far less complicated. You just give him the ball, watch how the batsmen get nervous, and rely on your wicketkeeper to keep Shane up to the mark. He has more patience than either Abdul Qadir or Mushtaq Ahmed and is more economical. Shane's line is so tight, he is so fast through the air, and he spins it so much that a batsman has to think very carefully about trying to drive him. You can try getting down the pitch to him – but remember, he's quick and he bowls a very good flipper. You can try sweeping him, but that's dangerous because he turns the ball away from the bat and a top edge is always likely.

Just imagine how England's fortunes would have been transformed in recent years if they'd had someone like Shane Warne available. Mike Atherton would probably have been knighted by now after winning back the Ashes at the first attempt! Shane is one cricketer who has been marvellous for the game of cricket and I hope we'll see a steady stream of young leg spinners coming through. I hope his shoulder holds out for a few more years, because I love watching him bowl. He must be one of the greatest bowlers of all time. His record is phenomenal. He's also a great guy with a terrific attitude to the responsibility to entertain.

WAQAR YOUNIS has been one of the most devastating bowlers I have seen, and he has been great for my career. It's a terrific boost to have another fast bowler firing away at the other end, especially when he is so different in style. I'm very grateful to Imran Khan for spotting him and giving him his chance, but Waqar was his own man after that. Early on he blasted out batsmen by sheer speed and reverse swing, and he was a sensation in county cricket. A marvellous sight as he roars in off that long run, he has put an enormous strain on his body. Recovering from two operations for stress fractures of the back underlines his physical bravery and huge self-belief. Waqar is physically very strong and he looks after his body as well as working hard on his technique in the nets. His action is so hard on his bowling boots that he tears them to shreds, dragging his back foot along the ground at the moment of delivery and hammering down his front foot just before releasing the ball. He gets through three pairs a season in an English summer, and they cost £400 a pair. I assume he has a sponsorship deal!

When Waqar is in rhythm he can be unplayable, but if not, he can get hammered. He relies on getting it just right after that surging, long run, and if the timing is astray he can lose his accuracy. Waqar has bowled at his peak in England, especially on dry wickets, and in Pakistan, where his speed through the air gets many trapped lbw on the front foot as they play forward on low, slow pitches. He has more trouble than me on the bouncy wickets encountered in Australia because he can be wayward and get carried away by seeing the ball explode. The new ball can distract him for the same reason, but he's learning all the while. He's more aware now, for example, that if you don't make the batsman play, you're not bowling well, even if it looks spectacular.

For the last few years some of us in the Pakistan camp have been telling him to think more about how to use the new ball, rather than charge in, aiming to blast them out. With the new ball you don't need to try different things, but Waqar was going for the yorker, the bouncer, and the one angled in at the rib cage. I settled for bowling just outside off-stump, trying to get the batsmen playing, saving the tricky stuff till the ball started to reverse swing. Waqar is now reining in his early aggression, thinking more about how to use the new ball more productively, and I believe that will prolong his career.

A strong-minded character, occasionally stubborn and outspoken, Waqar is basically a nice guy, and our personal relationship is now happy and supportive. Certainly he's been a very important foil for my bowling.

MALCOLM MARSHALL was the best fast bowler in my time. He had everything. Marshall was the only bowler who could completely outwit you with variations of pace from the same run-up; you rarely knew how fast the ball was until it was on you. His changes of pace on a slow wicket were remarkable. Living proof that you don't need to be tall to be a fast bowler, he could swing it both ways with old and new ball, was a master at reverse swing, and disconcerted everyone with a rapid bouncer that skidded through very swiftly at your head.

I'll never forget a spell from him towards the end of the Lahore Test of 1989. On a very slow pitch it was the fastest spell of bowling I have batted against. Imran and I were just blocking, trying to save the game, when Marshall came on for one final blast. Remember, this was a dead pitch. We were both dumped twice on our backsides by some deadly bouncers from the deceptively fast right arm. It was a major test of nerve and I was exhilarated to have survived it.

Marshall was a great thinker and strategist. He used the crease superbly to get different angles, and he was always altering his field, sometimes after every ball. He loved to probe a batsman's weakness, setting him up for the kill, letting him worry that the bowler's field changes meant he was on to him, about to pick him off. You could never relax when Malcolm Marshall was bowling. He didn't believe in the macho aspect of fast bowling – hurling down bouncers, trying physical intimidation, testing out your bravery. He was much more subtle, asking technical questions, accompanied by a cold stare.

Malcolm was our fast bowling coach for a season at Lancashire and he was a great help to me. For a time that year I couldn't get my inswinger going to the right-hander from around the wicket. That had been a delivery which had brought me lots of wickets over the years, and he spotted what was wrong as soon as I asked his advice. He told me to get my body more sideways, to cock my wrist before delivery, and to bowl it across my body. He also suggested I ran in quicker when I wanted to bowl the inswinger. It was the perfect diagnosis, and the inswinger returned. Just a matter of fine tuning, but typical of a supreme thinker. Malcolm Marshall would be my first choice if anyone wanted a fast bowling coach. If younger players are a little sceptical, just run a video of any Test match during Marshall's wonderful career.

VIV RICHARDS was not only a fabulous batsman, he was a wonderful sight on the field. Even though you must concentrate on your own efforts out in the middle, I never got tired of watching Viv come in to bat against us. He'd stroll in, chewing his gum, ready to stare at anyone who might threaten his place in the centre of the action. When he was really fired up, he'd bang down his bat loudly in the bowling crease after hitting you for four, then jam down hard on the top of the bat handle, as if to say 'It's my day, sunshine.' No one imposed himself more dramatically than Viv. He had presence, a great physique, and a level of performance that he maintained for a long time.

I found Viv a stimulating opponent, even though he would murder you if it was his day. You must raise your game against a player of such stature, otherwise you don't deserve to be out there playing for your country. His duels with Imran Khan were fantastic – two immensely proud cricketers, determined not to give an inch, with their egos highly visible. The sight of Imran gliding in against someone itching to smash him all over the ground was one of the most stirring memories of my career. I suppose honours worked out pretty even over the years, but the atmosphere is what sticks in my memory. That and Viv Richards' on side play. How he smacked good-length balls outside off-stump through mid-wicket like a rocket remains a mystery, and he rarely got pinned lbw. I don't expect to see again in my career someone bat and perform like Viv Richards. He was major box office.

SACHIN TENDULKAR could end up as the most successful batsman of the nineties. At the start of the decade he was just short of his seventeenth birthday, but I'd already seen enough to be certain he was set to be a star. He had just made his Test debut for India in the most testing of situations, on a tour to Pakistan, and he didn't look fazed at any stage. He batted at number six in difficult circumstances againt Imran, Waqar, Abdul Qadir, and myself and looked very much at home. Sachin made two fifties in the series and during one of them, at Sialkot, I tried to ruffle him with a barrage of bouncers. He wasn't put out at all by the assault and I ended up wasting a lot of energy and being warned by umpire John Holder.

Tendulkar is a classic example of the player being so good that his age is an irrelevance. India and Pakistan are the foremost exponents of this attitude, and other countries are at fault in not backing youth. Tendulkar's model correctness and calm strokeplay have made him one of world cricket's best batsmen and probably its wealthiest, and good luck to him. It's remarkable he has remained so balanced and modest with all the adulation heaped on him in his home country, and the fact that he has continued to bat so prolifically and attractively confirms a steely temperament. Sachin could easily break all international batting records if he keeps his hunger. He has everything a top batsman needs.

GRAHAM GOOCH is the only Englishman of my time I can call a great player, because none of the others have matched his consistency. The opener's job is the most difficult for a batsman because you can easily get undone by an unplayable delivery with the new ball, so you need to cash in when the luck is going your way. You need to be brave as well and keep your nerve. Graham Gooch did just that for years and years, all over the world, and never flinched. His was the prized England wicket above anyone else's, and I admired his competitiveness.

At Old Trafford in 1992, Waqar and I really bent our backs on the Saturday night trying to dismiss Gooch. We knew that if he went that evening, we'd have a great chance of enforcing the follow-on. He never buckled. It was a great duel on a quick wicket and Gooch was too good for us. In that same series he won the Leeds Test for England with a superb hundred. I beat him several times outside the off-stump with some unplayable deliveries, and he'd nod at me in appreciation. I'd swear at him in frustration, but I had to admire the way he made a fresh guard and played the next ball purely on its merits.

His appetite for runs and stamina for batting were remarkable.

Near the end of his career, when he was forty-two, he made 123 out of 248 for Essex at Old Trafford, and he didn't play a false shot. With that high backlift, a yorker would be the favourite to dismiss him, but one rarely got through. He wasn't just a specialist against fast bowling though. I've seen him hammer our leg spinners, Abdul Qadir and Mushtaq Ahmed, all over the place. Gooch led from the front and must have despaired sometimes that other England batsmen seemed incapable of following his example. Definitely the kind of batsman to play for your life.

CHAPTER 14

The Future

MISSING SO much cricket in 1997 was the worst time in my career, but at least the inactivity gave me time to think, to work out where my life and cricket were heading. It also gave the other parts of my body time to rest while the shoulder healed, recharged the mental batteries, and made me aware how precious are the periods when a sportsman isn't dogged by injury. I sat back and analysed how to improve my game, and see what else I could do for both Pakistan and Lancashire. A long lay-off isn't rec-ommended to anyone, but at least it gives you the opportunity to look at your prospects with some clarity and self-criticism. The day your ambition fades is the time to get out of your chosen sport, and I'm still a long way from that, despite the traumas of January 1988.

My shoulder problem had been dogging me on and off for a couple of years and I kept postponing surgery. When you play the amount of cricket I do, it's difficult to take off a chunk of time and you tell yourself it'll ease. The shoulder went completely in April 1997 during the Singer Cup final in Sharjah when I tried to bowl a bouncer. I saw a specialist out there, he told me to rest for a week, and when I returned to Old Trafford I was given the same advice. The shoulder was very painful, with swelling and internal bleeding. After a time I managed to get through a few Sunday League matches for Lancashire, but the problem flared up again in the championship game against Nottinghamshire. I'd bowled well in the first innings, taking three wickets in twenty overs, but there was a reaction and I just couldn't bowl the 'effort' ball later in the game. Lawrie Brown, our hard-working physiotherapist, said I'd need an operation. I was shattered, really downcast, having looked forward so much to playing a full season for Lancashire after missing the previous summer because of the Pakistan tour. Perhaps this would be the season when we won the title at last? If so, I wanted to be there. I was also embarrassed to be a well-paid overseas player who wasn't playing, thereby leaving Lancashire in the lurch.

In mid-July a London surgeon, Ian Bayley, put a camera in my shoulder and discovered that a tiny ball of bone was tilted into my shoulder ligaments. There was also some general wear and tear that wasn't serious. At the time I couldn't lift up my left shoulder, and I was in agony for about a month. I was taking eight painkillers a day, losing weight, and couldn't face food. In my darkest moments I thought my career was in jeopardy, but my wife, Huma, is such a positive person that she insisted I should look at the pluses: that my body was resting, and that I'd be raring to go once the operation had succeeded.

Huma was a tower of strength during that black period, especially as she was heavily pregnant with our first child. We ended up consoling each other at various stages, and my injury problems were put into perspective when she lay in labour for seventeen hours. I was more involved in the pregnancy than I ever expected to be. Attending ante-natal classes was an interesting experience, particularly as there is no such thing in Pakistan. I had a ringside seat to witness both the pain a brave mother has to go through and the birth of our son, Tahmoor. It was an emotional, exciting moment that will always stay with me. It was a miracle – there is no other word for it. When you see something like that, a painful shoulder doesn't seem quite so traumatic. My injury simplified matters in terms of being there for the birth, although I'm sure Lancashire would have been kind enough to allow me to be at the bedside even if I was playing somewhere else in the country for them. I'm sure the club would have understood that the birth of your first child is more important than cricket, if only for that memorable day. Even though Tahmoor is only three months old, I really miss being with my family even for a few days. I am looking forward to teaching my son cricket, if he shows an interest.

It was a good time to be at home for a prolonged period, to

appreciate being a father at last, and to think deeply about what I had achieved. The operation was a complete success and Ian Bayley reassured me I'd be as fit as ever once I'd rehabilitated properly and trained at a sensible pace. That was wise advice, because I'd been rash about injuries in the past. Lancashire were marvellous to me during this time. The players would ring me all the time and give me a great welcome whenever I turned up at Old Trafford to see them, but it's not the same as when you're playing – you feel a little on the outside, looking in. The club officials, especially John Bower and David Edmundson, were very sympathetic and Lawrie Brown assured me that I could call him anywhere at any time. Old Trafford has been like an extended family to me and I was very appreciative of all the concern shown, especially as I knew some of the members were starting to ask questions about my future prospects. In addition, we weren't having a good season and the criticism was becoming more vocal. It was obvious that my situation was troubling the cricket committee, and gradually leaks started to appear in the local press. The word was that they wanted Shane Warne to replace me as the overseas player for 1998. Now that would certainly appease the membership if Shane wanted to sign – a big 'if', that one – but what to do about me? I had another year of my contract to run, so would they pay that up, allowing me to go to another county? I desperately hoped not, because my heart was with Old Trafford and I couldn't face the prospect.

The uncertainty dragged on throughout August. The cricket committee tried a compromise: use me as a bowling coach and sign Shane Warne. The committee sympathetically pointed out that as I'd had a lot of cricket in recent years I might consider having a rest from playing in 1998. But, as I told them, I don't have the aptitude to be a coach. I'm an instinctive cricketer who wouldn't have the ability to have in-depth sessions with players, fine-tuning their techniques. I haven't put any great thought into coaching and I don't expect to be a coach when I retire from playing. I wanted to play for Lancashire in 1998, especially as I would miss the summer of 1999 with the World Cup being staged in England. Time was running out on my Lancashire career and I still wanted desperately to be part of a championship-winning side. I wasn't even sure that Shane Warne was totally committed to playing county cricket in

1998; he didn't need the money, and with Australia playing so much international cricket I was sure his board of control would have a few things to say on the subject. It was understandable that our cricket committee wanted to sort things our early, but I felt they were rushing things a little. I told them that I'd know very soon about my long-term fitness prospects, that I wouldn't leave them dangling in the air till the following March or April, and that, if the omens weren't good, I'd help find them a top replacement.

It was a worrying period for me, but finally the all-clear from the surgeon at the end of August convinced the cricket committee I'd be fine for 1998. They appointed me captain of Lancashire for the new season, a major boost to my morale after a difficult few months, so I now have a great deal to look forward to at Old Trafford. The club have also kindly granted me a benefit for 1998 in recognition of my services, which was greatly appreciated, and we have a new chairman who will be a great asset. Jack Simmons breezed into the job last September, and his first words to me were, 'Don't call me chairman, call me Simmo, like when we were players together,' and that's typical of him. Simmo was a great servant to the club as a player, and there's no better link between supporters and the dressing-room than this guy. He's infectious, optimistic, knows the game through and through, and appreciates the frustrations suffered in recent years by our supporters. We can't go wrong with Simmo in charge.

My inactivity for Lancashire was repeated with Pakistan, and that was doubly frustrating. When I finally gave in to the shoulder problem, I felt that I was near to getting the job right as Pakistan captain. My experience on tour in England had pleased me, and I was gratified by many kind words in the English media about how we had conducted ourselves. It *was* possible to win while playing with a smile on your face. I wanted to build on that philosophy. Over the next few months after the England tour, we continued to consolidate our good reputation. We won Tests at home against New Zealand and Zimbabwe, triumphed in the Sharjah Trophy, and surprised many good judges in Australia by winning the World Series tournament for the first time in sixteen years. That was accomplished with a very young side that entertained and bubbled attractively, and the home crowds really took to us. When

Australia surprisingly failed to qualify for the final, we got all the home support against the West Indies. As captain, I was proud and very happy about that. Little did I realise what was in store!

My form was also very encouraging before my injury. I missed the New Zealand series after the shoulder flared up again, but I picked up the man of the match award in both Tests against Zimbabwe. The second, in Faisalabad, was for taking ten wickets in the match, which we won inside three days by ten wickets, but the first Test – well, that was very special for me. I actually scored 257 not out, and no one was more astonished than me. I made the highest score by a number eight batsman in Test history and my twelve sixes were the most ever in a Test innings by a single batsman. One more statistic: Saqlain Mushtaq and I added 313 for the seventh wicket, another record in Tests. It was absolutely amazing. Two things in particular will stick in my mind as long as I live: just how tired I was after batting for more than eight hours, and Waqar Younis being bowled first ball after sitting with his pads on all that time waiting for me or Saqlain to be dismissed!

Now I'm sure that when the news from Sheikhpura went around the world, most cricket fans must have thought it was a misprint. Perhaps Wasim Akram had scored 57 not out, but not 257 not out? Up till then, I'd been occasionally successful as a batsman in low-scoring, tight situations that brought out my competitive instinct, but often I'd got myself out through an indiscriminate slog stemming from a lack of concentration. Yet I'd been thinking harder about doing myself justice as a batsman, telling myself that one Test hundred in over a decade wasn't very impressive. If I could get in early enough in the innings, with time to spare to build a knock, I might start compiling useful runs and play like a proper all-rounder. My chance came against Zimbabwe in that first Test. Their leg spinner, Paul Strang, had bowled very well to reduce us to 183 for 6 when I walked in. The situation cried out for boldness to me, especially as the Sheikhpura ground has some inviting straight boundaries that aren't very long. I decided to hit through the line, and the straight sixes arrived. When Saqlain Mushtaq came in, he made it clear he too fancied himself for a long stay. I told him to play his natural game, so he blocked for hours and we kept laughing at the end of each over. He was great company.

I got to my century and double hundred with a six. For the first, I middled the straight drive perfectly and the ball soared away like the perfect golf drive off the tee. The second came from a pick-up between long-on and mid-wicket, and it went out of the stadium. Fantastic! One of my dreams in cricket had always been to score a double hundred at some stage, even if it was just a friendly match, and here I'd done it captaining my country in a Test match. On top of all that, I hit the record number of sixes. I was indebted to Ijaz Ahmed for that, because when I was on nine he sent out a message to tell me I needed three more. So I waited for the right deliveries and away they went. At least three of the sixes were mishits and I thought, 'Oh, I've gone', but they had enough power to get over the rope. Paul Strang was unlucky not to get more wickets at a cheaper rate; he is a great trier. I might even have made three hundred if the declaration hadn't been imminent. That was only right – the game's result was more important than individual glory – so when I told Saqlain to get a move on, the wickets started to clatter and I was left unbeaten.

Not before that priceless moment with Waqar, though. When he joined me in the middle, I told him: 'This bowler's swinging it in, so watch the yorker.' Now Waqar fancies himself as a batsman, and he probably thought the bowling couldn't be that special if I'd hit a double hundred. So he just grunted at me and was bowled comprehensively, first ball, by Guy Whittall's perfect inswinging yorker. This after having to watch me hit sixes for hour after hour! I couldn't look at Waqar as he dragged himself back to the pavilion, and I burst out laughing when we finally met up in the dressing-room. For the rest of our careers, I'll be able to give him advice when we're batting together and suggest he listens to me!

That innings of mine certainly got me thinking. I was pleased that I'd got the big score when we were in trouble. It didn't matter too much to me that Zimbabwe weren't a great bowling side because it's all a matter of confidence, and if you're feeling good about your batting the opponents aren't massively important. I learned from that innings that you can't hit every ball a long way, that you must wait and be selective. I don't want to finish my Test career as a slogger, a hit-and-miss batsman who can't concentrate. I want to move up the order. If you bat at six or seven rather than eight or nine, you do play more responsibly. The mental and physical demands are great, though, if you want to be an opening bowler who bats in the middle order. I don't know how Imran and Ian Botham did it for so many years. After that double hundred, I could barely put one foot in front of the other for a couple of days. My hamstrings and back ached because I'd been using different muscles for hour after hour. I was also mentally drained after having to think about where the fielders were placed, wondering whether to play off the front or back foot, whether I should have got two rather than a single for that shot, and what is the wicket doing? With bowling, it is predominantly instinctive with me. I run up and bowl, and if I have a bad over I can retrieve the situation in a few minutes' time. One mistake as a batsman in a Test match, and the chances are you'll be out. No wonder Javed Miandad used to say that batting was hard work. It can also be very satisfying, and I now want to bat more consistently.

Winning that one-day series in Australia was a fantastic achievement. We were without several senior players, yet we bonded superbly, and older guys like Moin Khan and Ijaz Ahmed set a great example. Our fielding was superb, stemming from some enjoyable practice sessions I had learned about at Lancashire under David Lloyd. The oldies would take on the youngsters and the losers had to do press-ups in the dressing-room, cheered on by everybody. That great team spirit carried us through some big challenges, and a measure of our moral was the successful way in which we defended small totals to squeeze out narrow victories. In Hobart, Australia bowled us out for 149 but they were dismissed for 120, and in the Melbourne final we bowled West Indies out for 103 after we'd managed only 165. Those sorts of wins are very satisfying to a captain, because determination and total commitment are vital in such tight situations.

The Australian public took to us in a big way because we were obviously enjoying our cricket out there, and our varied bowling attack meant we were interesting to watch. I also made sure that all the younger Pakistan players learned about dealing with the media, so that we were accessible to the public. In the end, all the boys came to enjoy being interviewed because that meant we were doing well. It also helped to continue the rehabilitation of our image throughout world cricket. It caused a big sensation that Australia didn't contest the finals, because they certainly fancied their chances, but the support we got from the public was very gratifying to me. It was just as pleasing as our reception a few months earlier in England.

Those two tours have convinced me that Pakistan now has a great chance to become the best side in the world. Forget the established players; there'll be a time when we're all out of it, inside five years or so. I'm so excited about the quality of our younger players. It's almost a cliché now to talk about Pakistanis springing from obscurity to become international stars overnight, but it seems to be happening more and more. I can barely keep up with it all, and I'm the national captain.

On that successful Australian trip I was so impressed by four players all under the age of twenty who looked as if they'd been playing for us for years. There was Shahid Afridi, who was voted player of the finals for his uninhibited batting, yet just a few months earlier he was a leg-spin bowler of great promise with no pretensions to batting. I first saw him in Kenya where he replaced the injured Mushtaq. We knew he had bowled impressively for Pakistan under-19s in the West Indies, and towards the end of nets one evening I asked him if he batted. He said he'd like to, and proceeded to smash all the bowlers around. So we made a note of him and he didn't let us down in the Sharjah Trophy. Coming in at number three against Sri Lanka, he hit the fastest hundred cricket has ever seen in one-day internationals. Going on to Australia, he opened the batting and was a very successful pinch-hitter as well as an effective bowler, with an impressive quicker ball. He didn't seem fazed by any of the demands put on him. All this at the age of eighteen.

Away from cricket, though, Shahid needs guidance. He was involved in a distasteful incident on a plane coming back from Sri Lanka which led to a complaint about his behaviour from three ladies who said they'd been pestered by him during the flight. Our board of control cracked down hard on him. Part of his problem is that he didn't have as good an education as many of us, so he needs advice on how to cope with all the attention at such a tender age. He may be mature as a cricketer, but he's still young in the ways of the world. There's no doubt about his all-round talents, though.

Mohammad Zahid also impressed many on that Australian trip with some genuinely quick spells, bowling several hostile overs in particular in Brisbane against Brian Lara which drew high praise on television from Tony Cosier and Ian Chappell. They reckoned Zahid was as quick as Waqar has ever been, and that made many take notice. When I pulled out of the New Zealand Test at Rawalpindi with my shoulder injury, he came in for his first Test and took 11 for 130 in the match. In the nets he had been very fast, but very wayward. There were times when he and the batsman didn't know where the ball would pitch, but Zaheer Abbas, his loyal mentor, was a great help. In the Test match he was devastating on a slow pitch.

In that same series, Mohammad Wasim scored a hundred on his Test debut in dramatic circumstances. He had made nought in the first innings and came in second time around with Pakistan on 42 for 5. Wasim ended 109 not out from a total of 231 playing his natural game, totally unintimidated by the situation. He was equally effective in Australia, particularly in that low-scoring game in Hobart against Australia when he made fifty-four out of 149, easily the highest score of the day. His forty-one in the second final at Melbourne was made against Curtly Ambrose with his tail up, and it proved a vital contribution to a total of 165.

Then young Shahid Nazir came good just when we needed a performance from our fourth seamer. With such a low total to chase, we needed to bowl the West Indies out. Waqar Younis had made important early breakthroughs, but as long as Brian Lara was in they were favourites. Shahid got him caught behind after he'd been batting for an hour and a half, and then he got Jimmy Adams and Phil Simmons. He ended up with 4 for 13 from ten overs, a nerveless effort from someone so inexperienced.

Those four young players will have learned a great deal from being thrown in at the deep end over those few months. In comparison with Hassan Raza, they're almost veterans. I picked Raza for his first Test at the age of fourteen years and 227 days, and everyone in the rest of world cricket must have thought we were crazy. Again, credit must go to Zaheer Abbas for spotting his talent and persuading the selectors to take a chance on the boy. And he was a boy, despite our own board saying they doubted that after taking a bone scan on his wrist. I'm no medical expert, but he was in the appropriate class at school for his official age, and I know that he had to write to his headmaster for permission to play in the Faisalabad Test.

It wasn't such a great risk to take. We would have thought long and hard about putting him in against one of the major Test sides, but Zimbabwe weren't the strongest of units and we wanted to see how he would cope with the pressure. I had seen him playing a few months earlier in England when he scored eighty at Lord's against India in the final of the Under-Fifteen World Cup Challenge, and he looked a high-class player that day. Zaheer's judgement could be trusted, so we gave him his chance and he made Test history as the youngest ever debutant. I batted with him for a time and was amazed at his mature confidence. He said to me: 'Come on, captain – I'm here with you, just relax and enjoy it.' This was my seventy-second Test match, by the way, and this schoolboy was geeing me up! He played very well, making twenty-seven, and his education continued on the 'A' tour to England in the summer of 1997, where he again looked a major young talent.

And to those who say we were wrong to play him so early, I say Mushtaq Mohammad. He was the record-holder before Hassan Raza, making his Test debut at fifteen years and 124 days, and that experience didn't do him any harm. Mushy became a great player for us for twenty years, and Hassan could easily do the same. If they have the technique and natural ability, you must find out as soon as possible if they have the requisite heart, fighting qualities, and mental steel against the big boys.

We do seem to have hit a winning streak lately with our gambles on young players. We continued our good form as talent-spotters in the home series against South Africa, late in 1997. Again we made Test history, with two players scoring hundreds on their Test debuts. Azhar Mahmood, coming in at number eight, became the first Pakistani to score a hundred and then fifty on his Test debut and he also shared in a last-wicket stand of 151 that equalled the Test record. He then opened the bowling with Waqar Younis, a useful start to an international career at the age of twenty-two. The opening batsman Ali Naqvi also made a remarkable hundred at the age of twenty, after just three months in the first-class game. Earlier in the year he had turned up at the Pakistan camp with a letter from his boss saying that the young man was good enough to play for his country, and could he have a trial? Our new coach, Haroon Rashid, was open-minded enough to let him have a net, and he impressed. Soon after that, he's scoring a hundred in his first Test match. Would England have treated that young man so tolerantly?

I hope that this faith in youth will be one of my most enduring legacies from my time as Pakistan's captain. I didn't want the senior side to be a cosy clique, with players living on past glories, jealous of competition. I wanted to see young, successful players taking on opponents with vigour and boldness, the sort of positive attitude that's appreciated by crowds all over the world. I believe that the senior side has the bowlers to win on any surface, anywhere. No other country has the variety of our senior quartet – Waqar, myself, Mushtaq, and Saqlain – and I hope we'll prove that in the next year or so if we can overcome the various bouts of infighting and unfounded allegations about bribes. Yet when we start to fade away, I'm very confident that some of the younger players I've mentioned will replace us easily enough. We could be entering a golden age of Pakistan cricket, and I believe our reputation will remain high, with our behaviour improved noticeably.

Behaviour on the field generally will steadily improve as the Test-playing countries continue to understand each other more easily. Since the introduction of third-country umpires and match referees to hand out fines and/or suspensions, there has been a reduction in the kind of spats that disfigure cricket. Pakistan's players have been more culpable than most in the past, as I've pointed out already in this book, but I feel we're moving on the right lines now, so that misunderstandings don't fester too long and turn into outright hositility. I'm very encouraged at the decision of the International Cricket Council to hold an annual meeting between the Test captains, where thorny topics can be thrashed out. The captain's views will then be reported to the ICC's cricket committee, so at last there will be regular dialogue between players and administrators. I was part of the first meeting just before the World Cup in 1996, and the following summer we met up again in London for a productive session that lasted a full day. It was a great chance to get to know the other captains; the only ones I knew well were Mike Atherton, Courtney Walsh, and Mark Taylor. That sort of relationship must give us a great chance of better understanding between opposing sides, because the captains ought to be the ones to set the tone. When you're up against guys like Athers and Mark, you know you'll have a hard but sporting series, with no quarter given on the field and the hand of friendship offered afterwards. That's the way I've always wanted to play my cricket.

During the meeting we all expressed differing views, but the discussions were really thorough and enjoyable. Some of us – like Mark Taylor, Hansie Cronje, and myself – said we should have as many bouncers as possible in Tests instead of just two an over, and leave it to the umpires to decide what was excessive. We believe the ability of batsmen to play the short-pitched delivery is on the wane in Test cricket, because they are being protected by this rule. It's like saying you can't bowl more than two yorkers in an over – it takes away the surprise element. We were outvoted on that one. The question of TV replays was also discussed, and the majority view was that it should be available to the umpire for disputed catches, run-outs, and stumpings. Athers thought that would be taking authority away from the umpire, but he lost out to the general view that if the technology is there, then use it. All the captains agreed that former first-class cricketers who want to become umpires should be fast-tracked, as they are in South Africa. We talked about the sheer volume of international cricket and the amount of travelling in between games. I said that back-to-back matches with gaps in between were preferable, and that one-dayers should come after the Test series. That was generally agreed. We all thought it a good idea to use floodlights for Tests when the light is bad. The spectactors have paid good money to be there and shouldn't be frustrated by bad light. The general view was that behaviour had improved in the past two years, and that referees were doing a good job. When our players are banned, we do take notice.

The meeting was very constructive. It was chaired by the ICC chief executive David Richards, with other executive officials attending; we had a proper agenda and minutes were compiled. It will be a regular annual meeting in London, before the full ICC gathering, and I feel sure that the players' views will be heard more sympathetically from now on. I'm also sure that working relationships between captains will improve as a result.

So the signs are good for international cricket. Despite my recent problems, there are still a few ambitions left for me. I believe I could play at the top level until at least the year 2000, now that I'm convinced my injury problems are behind me and I'm more aware of how to look after my body. I'm just as committed to high standards as ever, still striving to win trophies for my sides. I'd love to see Lancashire win the championship, for the first time outright since 1934. After their loyalty to me, I owe them all the commitment I can dredge up, all the inspiration I can find. I was thrilled to be asked to captain Lancashire for the 1998 season, something I'd always wanted to do on a full-time basis before I left the club. Having done it at various stages, I feel I have the respect of the players and will know how to handle them. I won't have rules that apply to every player, without exception. For example, if someone has taken a lot of wickets or scored a hundred the day before, they don't have to be running around the outfield an hour before start of play. They can come later, and be fresh.

For Pakistan, I believe we have an excellent chance of winning the World Cup in England in 1999, provided we get some stability. We have the flair, the matchwinning bowlers, and we love playing international cricket in England. It would also be wonderful to return to Test series on a regular basis with India. That's the big series for any Pakistani cricketer, yet we haven't been there for Tests since 1989/90 due to political tensions.

As for me, I fancy a crack at Kapil Dev's world record of 434 wickets in Tests. I'm not a slave to statistics, but some records are very special and that one might just be possible if I can keep fit for three years or so and regain my place. With the bat, it's time I scored more runs and got myself up the batting order. Sheikhpura in October 1996 will by my inspiration! If all those things happen, I'll be ecstatic. If not, I'll still look back on my great good fortune.

Coping with the
Mental Pressure

M Y WIFE, *Huma, and I have know each other for ten years and have been married since October 1993. She has been a rock to me in so many ways, not least in getting me mentally strong for challenges on the field. People don't realise how important mind games are to a top sportsman. Of course natural ability gives you a start, but a strong mental approach is also vital. You can't perform on talent alone at the highest level, and Huma has helped channel me into the right psychological areas that allow me to do justice to my abilities. She is a qualified hypnotherapist and psychotherapist, with a degree from Pakistan in Psychology, English Literature and Europan History, and a Psychology degree from Unversity College, London. Huma has also worked informally with my Pakistan team-mates Saeed Anwar and Saqlain Mushtaq, and she has clients in both Pakistan and England. She is a good deal cleverer than me, as you're about to find out!*

When assessing the qualities of someone so outstanding in sport, you have to take talent for granted. Mental steel is sixty per cent of the equation, in my opinion. You need the psychological skills to control yourself in a match context, irrespective of natural ability. If you're in charge mentally, enjoying the challenges, then the juices of natural talent flow unhindered and you do yourself justice. Then it's a case of being strong enough psychologically to recreate your successes in your mind and then repeat them on the field, in the flesh. The world-class performers also set themselves imposing standards and keep living up to them. Consistency is more of a mental thing than just turning on the tap of your talent. I think Wasim has managed that for most of his career, and he is now psychologically so strong that he should carry on maintaining his high standards, so long as his body holds out.

I knew nothing about cricket when I met Wasim, and I don't know a great deal more now, which I believe is a help to him. I see my role as one of indirect hypnosis, using relaxation techniques that are part of hypnotherapy. Knowing little about cricket is beneficial, because it saves getting sidetracked by technical detail. My best work with Wasim comes the night before he's due to play, and only when he's requested a relaxation session. I never force it on him, so he can either turn to me if he's particularly keyed up, or not bother.

Image-building and positive affirmations are the main parts of my technique. They would be helpful to any sportsman and are quite simple to do. I reaffirm positives and eliminate all negative aspects. I'll ask him to imagine a previous situation in a game when he's been successful, and suggest he incorporates that into the following day's play. Never talk about the opposition or your team-mates; home in on yourself and your successes. That was particularly vital in those awful weeks after the Sharjah Tournament at the end of 1997.

It's never a case of saying directly, 'Close your eyes,' it's more a matter of coaxing gently. I'll say, 'If you'd like to relax now, and think of a place where you're comfortable and happy. Then, if you would, tell me about a time when you've performed well.' Wasim will be wide awake at this juncture, but I'll be hoping that he'll be visibly relaxing. The place which I want him to visualise doesn't have to be a cricket ground; he's very fond of the sea, or the woods, indeed anywhere out in the open, enjoying fresh air. Indirect hypnosis is all about encouragement; there's no compulsion – that's why it's best to use conciliatory terms like 'If you would', or 'If you'd care to'. The best work I do with clients is when they're awake, relaxed, and susceptible. The voice tone must be soft and even. It's good to emphasise certain words that don't jar and to insert pieces of factual information at times. So, when Wasim has started to visualise a day when he has performed well, I can say, 'That was the day when you took eight wickets.' I'll say, 'Imagine you're out there, on the pitch, in front of all those people.' Then I'll try to get him to explain his emotions that day, while underlining his success. The idea is to tap into that feeling of achievement and well-being so that he'll be able to channel those positive thoughts into the next day's play. A lot of golfers approach an important round in the same way.

On the eve of the 1995 Benson and Hedges Cup final, Wasim was very tense for some reason. So we worked in the team hotel and I asked him to summon up an image that he liked. 'The sea and the wind coming in towards me,' he replied. I said, 'Would you tell me please what you want to do tomorrow?', and he answered, 'I want to get five wickets. I want to be the best all-rounder in the world.' After about twenty minutes he was so relaxed he could barely lift his arms, and his eyes looked very heavy. Then I said, 'If you would like to wake up slowly, please,' and he slept like a baby that night. There isn't a happy ending to this story though. Wasim injured his groin the next day and was expensive when he bowled, but I'd done my job! He's the one who has to bowl the overs!

Until the shocking match-fixing allegations caused Wasim such heartache, he had managed to ensure he wasn't taking the game home with him. In the past he has got down at times, but I've worked hard with him to channel the positive aspects of his career into productive repetition. I'll keep maximising his potential as a cricketer. When he talks about the need to be more consistent as a batsman, I'll agree and point out that this is well within his poten-tial, because he has already been good enough to score 257 not out in a Test match. So he can do it again. It's never a good time to bring in doubts about such an ambition, like reminding him of how many overs he has to bowl and that he might be too tired to be able to concentrate for very long when batting. You must always affirm that anything is possible.

Wasim has that strong mindset. If he has a bad day, he'll talk to me about it – but only if he brings the subject up – and then move on. He no longer broods on failure. He always strives to go one better, wanting five wickets next time rather than four, or relishing his professional rivalry with Waqar Younis. Wasim works better under pressure, turning out good performances when the team really needs him. Captaincy had brought that out of him even more. Perhaps the wheel will spin his way again when he's convinced the public of his innocence over the bribes slur, and he'll be captain again. Whatever happens, he'll remain positive. I keep insisting that everything is for the best and that he'll come out of this ordeal stronger.

Wasim Akram's Career Record

Figures correct to 15 December, 1997

CAREER HIGHLIGHTS

1984–85	Nov 9: First-class debut, aged 18 years 159 days, for BCCP Patron's XI v New Zealanders, taking 7–50 in the first innings
	Nov 23: Debut for Pakistan, in limited-overs international v New Zealand at Faisalabad
	Jan 25: Test debut v New Zealand at Auckland
1987	May 2: Played first match in UK as a member of the Pakistan Touring Team – v Surrey at The Oval
	July 4: 100th first-class wicket: M W Gatting (2nd innings) Pakistan v England, Third Test at Headingley
	August 11: Appendix removed
1987–88	Dec 7: Flu caused him to miss the Second Test v England
1988	May 5: Lancashire debut v Nottinghamshire at Trent Bridge
	May 8: Sunday debut v Nottinghamshire at Trent Bridge
	May 10: Benson & Hedges debut v Derbyshire at Liverpool
	May 28: Scored first first-class hundred v Somerset at Old Trafford
	June 22: NatWest debut v Lincolnshire at Old Trafford
	July 20/22: Hat trick v Surrey at Southport: Greig, Medlycott and Feltham
	Aug 1: Groin strain, which resulted in an operation. This caused him to miss the rest of the season. He arrived late in Pakistan and missed the West Indies series
1988–89	Jan 18: Broke down with hairline crack in a pelvic bone in the match at New Plymouth and returned to Pakistan
1989	Aug 22: 200th first-class wicket: D Byas (2nd innings) Lancashire v Yorkshire at Old Trafford
	50 wickets in a season (1): 63 wickets @ 17.73

1989–90	Oct 14: Hat trick v West Indies at Sharjah – Dujon, Marshall and Ambrose Jan 13: 100th Test wicket: T M Alderman Pakistan v Australia at Melbourne Jan 22: 1st Test hundred v Australia at Adelaide May 4: Hat trick v Australia at Sharjah – Hughes, Rackemann and Alderman
1990–91	Dec 8: 300th first-class wicket: P J L Dujon (2nd innings) Pakistan v West Indies, Third Test at Lahore
1991	Jul 24: Removed from attack by Umpire Plews for persistent intimidatory bowling: Lancashire v Warwickshire at Old Trafford. Fined £1,000 by Lancashire 50 wickets in a season (2): 56 wickets @ 22.33
1992	Jun 18: 400th first-class wicket: G A Gooch Pakistan v England, Second Test at Lord's 50 wickets in a season (3): 82 wickets @ 16.21
1992–93	Jan 5: Reached 1,000 Test runs and therefore the double: Pakistan v New Zealand at Hamilton Apr 16: Captained Test for the first time, 47 days before 27th birthday: Pakistan v West Indies at Port-of-Spain
1993	Jun 7: 500th first-class wicket: D J Bicknell Lancashire v Surrey at The Oval 50 wickets in a season (4): 59 wickets @ 19.27
1993–94	Dec 14: Won first Test as captain: Pakistan v Zimbabwe at Rawalpindi Feb 10: 200th Test wicket: T E Blain Pakistan v New Zealand, First Test at Auckland Feb 20: Best Test bowling: 7–119 v New Zealand at Wellington
1994	May 28: 600th first-class wicket: K A Parsons (2nd innings) Lancashire v Somerset at Southport
1995	Jun 26: 700th first-class wicket: P M Such (2nd innings) Lancashire v Essex at Old Trafford 50 wickets in a season (5): 81 wickets @ 19.72
1996	Aug 5: 800th first-class wicket: D G C Ligertwood Pakistanis v Durham at Chester-le-Street Aug 12: Reached 5,000 first-class runs in second innings Second Test v England at Headingley Aug 26: 300th Test wicket: A D Mullally Pakistan v England, Third Test at The Oval Aug 31: Played 200th Limited-overs International match

1996–97   Sep 29: 300th L/O International wicket: D L Houghton
           Pakistan v Zimbabwe at Quetta
           Oct 18/19/20: Scored highest Test and first-class score (257*)
           v Zimbabwe at Sheikhupura from 370 balls and 12 sixes, a
           record for a Test innings. His partnership of 313 with Saqlain
           Mushtaq (79) is a record for the 8th wicket for all Tests
           Dec 4: Reached 2,000 L/O International runs v New Zealand
           at Gujranwala
           April: Injured and missed the two Tests v Sri Lanka

1997   Shoulder injury restricted first team appearances to one match
           v Nottinghamshire at Old Trafford May 15–17

1997–98   Oct 6: Injured and missed First Test v South Africa at
           Rawalpindi
           Nov 17: Re-appointed as captain and led Pakistan to a three-
           nil series win over West Indies, the first time they had
           registered such a loss since 1928
           Jan 6: Resignation as captain reported

TEST CAPTAINCY RECORD

Captain 17   Won 9   Lost 4   Drawn 4

1.	1992–93	West Indies	1	Port-of-Spain	Lost by 204 runs
2.			2+	Bridgetown	Lost by ten wickets
3.			3	St John's	Drawn
4.	1993–94	Zimbabwe	2	Rawalpindi	Won by 52 runs[1]
5.			3	Lahore	Drawn
6.	1995–96	Australia	1	Brisbane	Lost by an innings and 126 runs
7.			2	Hobart	Lost by 155 runs
8.			3	Sydney	Won by 74 runs
9.		New Zealand	1+	Christchurch	Won by 161 runs
10.	1996	England	1	Lord's	Won by 164 runs
11.			2	Headingley	Drawn
12.			3	Oval	Won by nine wickets
13.	1996–97	Zimbabwe	1	Sheikhupura	Drawn
14.			2	Faisalabad	Won by ten wickets
15.	1997–98	West Indies	1	Peshawar	Won by an innings and 19 runs
16.			2+	Rawalpindi	Won by an innings and 29 runs
17.			3	Karachi	Won by ten wickets[2]

+ Won the toss and invited the opposition to bat

[1]Broke little finger in Sharjah on 2.11.1993 and missed First Test
[2]Injured shoulder and missed two Tests v New Zealand and two Tests v Sri Lanka

LIMITED-OVERS INTERNATIONAL CAPTAINCY RECORD
Captain 72   Won 43   Lost 28   Drawn 1

TEST MATCH SUMMARY

+ denotes in Pakistan

Season	Opponent	M	I	NO	HS	Runs	Av	100	50	Ct
1984–85	NZ	2	4	3	8*	9	9.00	–	–	–
1985–86	SL+	3	2	1	5*	9	9.00	–	–	1
	SL	3	4	0	19	30	7.50	–	–	–
1986–87	WI+	2	4	0	66	67	16.75	–	1	–
	Ind	5	6	1	62	89	17.80	–	1	2
1987	Eng	5	4	0	43	80	20.00	–	–	4
1987–88	Eng+	2	2	0	40	77	38.50	–	–	–
	WI	3	5	1	38	49	12.25	–	–	1
1989–90	Ind+	4	3	0	30	58	19.33	–	–	1
	Aus	3	5	0	123	197	39.40	1	1	2
1990–91	NZ+	2	2	0	28	29	14.50	–	–	1
	WI+	3	5	1	38	72	18.00	–	–	–
1991–92	SL+	3	3	1	54	87	43.50	–	1	–
1992	Eng	4	7	1	45*	118	19.66	–	–	–
1992–93	NZ	1	2	0	27	42	21.00	–	–	–
	WI	3	5	0	29	44	8.80	–	–	4
1993–94	Zim+	2	3	1	16*	42	21.00	–	–	1
	NZ	3	3	0	35	57	19.00	–	–	–
1994–95	SL	2	2	0	37	49	24.50	–	–	2
	Aus+	2	4	1	45*	93	31.00	–	–	1
	SA	1	2	0	41	52	26.00	–	–	–
	Zim	3	5	0	27	51	10.20	–	–	1
1995–96	SL+	2	3	0	36	64	21.33	–	–	2
	Aus	3	6	0	33	68	11.33	–	–	2
	NZ	1	2	0	19	21	10.50	–	–	–
1996	Eng	3	5	1	40	98	24.50	–	–	1
1996–97	Zim+	2	2	1	257*	292	292.00	1	–	1
1997–98	SA+	2	2	0	9	11	5.50	–	–	2
	WI+	3	3	0	11	16	5.33	–	–	2
TOTALS		**77**	**105**	**13**	**257***	**1971**	**21.42**	**2**	**4**	**31**

COUNTRY BY COUNTRY

		M	I	NO	HS	Runs	Av	100	50	Ct
New Zealand		9	13	3	35	158	15.80	–	–	1
Sri Lanka		13	14	2	54	239	19.91	–	1	5
West Indies		14	22	2	66	248	12.40	–	1	7
India		9	9	1	62	147	18.37	–	1	3
England		14	18	2	45*	373	23.31	–	–	5
Australia		8	15	1	123	358	25.57	1	1	5
Zimbabwe		7	10	2	257*	385	48.12	1	–	3
South Africa		3	4	0	41	63	15.75	–	–	2
HOME		32	38	6	257*	917	28.65	1	2	12
OVERSEAS		45	67	7	62	1054	17.56	1	2	19
TOTALS		**77**	**105**	**13**	**257***	**1971**	**21.42**	**2**	**4**	**31**

TEST MATCH SUMMARY

Overs	Mdns	Runs	Wkts	Av	BB	5wI	10wM	S/R
93.4	21	233	12	19.41	5–56	2	1	46.83
103.5	31	251	8	31.37	2–17	–	–	77.87
97.3	35	204	8	25.50	4–55	–	–	73.12
37	5	112	6	18.66	6–91	1	–	37.00
159.2	30	413	13	31.76	5–96	1	–	73.53
180.4	38	464	16	29.00	4–111	–	–	67.75
40.1	7	102	2	51.00	2–64	–	–	120.50
117	22	319	11	29.00	4–73	–	–	63.81
204.4	50	551	18	30.61	5–101	1	–	68.22
135.4	37	318	17	18.70	6–62	3	1	47.88
78.5	24	162	10	16.20	4–44	–	–	47.30
106	12	298	21	14.19	5–28	1	–	30.28
85	21	211	6	35.16	3–71	–	–	85.00
168.5	36	462	21	22.00	6–67	2	–	48.23
53	13	111	8	13.87	5–45	1	–	39.75
108.1	17	358	9	39.77	4–75	–	–	72.11
76.2	14	203	11	18.45	5–65	1	–	41.63
159.4	41	431	25	17.24	7–119	2	1	38.32
75.2	24	175	13	13.46	5–43	1	–	34.76
70.5	10	200	9	22.22	5–64	1	–	47.22
59	16	166	4	41.50	2–53	–	–	88.50
132.2	31	313	13	24.07	5–43	1	–	61.07
43	12	110	9	12.22	5–55	1	–	28.66
122.4	32	273	14	19.50	4–50	–	–	52.57
35.5	7	84	5	16.80	5–53	1	–	43.00
128	29	350	11	31.81	3–67	–	–	69.81
71.4	21	180	11	16.36	6–48	1	1	39.09
40	9	114	6	19.00	4–42	–	–	40.00
107.1	30	294	17	17.29	4–42	–	–	37.82
2891.1	**675**	**7462**	**334**	**22.34**	**7–119**	**21**	**4**	**51.93**
421	106	1021	60	17.01	7–119	6	2	42.09
404.4	123	951	44	21.61	5–43	2	–	56.54
475.2	86	1381	64	21.57	6–91	2	–	44.56
364	80	964	31	31.09	5–96	2	–	67.93
517.4	110	1378	50	27.56	6–67	2	–	62.12
329.1	79	791	40	19.77	6–62	4	1	49.37
280.2	66	696	35	19.88	6–48	3	1	48.05
99	25	280	10	28.00	4–42	–	–	59.40
1064.3	246	2788	134	20.80	6–48	7	1	47.66
1826.4	429	4674	200	23.37	7–119	14	3	54.80
2891.1	**675**	**7462**	**334**	**22.34**	**7–119**	**21**	**4**	**51.93**

SUMMARY OF ALL FIRST-CLASS MATCHES

+ Pakistan seasons including domestic cricket
Note: English seasons are for Lancashire unless noted

Season	Venue	M	I	NO	HS	Runs	Av	100	50	Ct
+1984–85	Pak	2	2	0	9	9	4.50	–	–	2
	NZ	3	5	4	8*	15	15.00	–	–	1
	SL	1	1	1	12*	12	–	–	–	–
+1985–86	Pak (SL)	6	5	1	8	22	5.50	–	–	4
	SL	5	5	0	19	34	6.80	–	–	1
1986–87	Pak (WI)	2	4	0	66	67	16.75	–	1	–
	Ind	6	7	2	62	90	18.00	–	1	3
1987	Pak in UK	14	11	2	59*	245	27.22	–	1	7
1987–88	Pak (Eng)	2	2	0	40	77	38.50	–	–	–
	WI	4	7	2	56*	121	24.20	–	1	1
1988		10	18	2	116*	496	31.00	1	3	2
1988–89	Aus	1	2	0	19	25	12.50	–	–	1
1989		13	20	3	49	350	20.58	–	–	3
1989–90	Pak (Ind)	4	3	0	30	58	19.33	–	–	1
	Aus	3	5	0	123	197	39.40	1	1	2
1990		8	11	0	32	135	12.27	–	–	–
1990–91	Pak (NZ/WI)	5	7	1	38	101	16.83	–	–	1
1991		14	19	2	122	471	27.70	1	1	5
1991–92	Pak (SL)	3	3	1	54	87	43.50	–	1	–
	Aus	2	3	0	30	70	23.33	–	–	–
1992	Pak in UK	14	18	3	45*	299	19.93	–	–	5
+1992–93	Pak	1	2	0	14	18	9.00	–	–	–
	Aus/NZ	2	3	0	27	45	15.00	–	–	1
	WI	5	7	0	29	64	9.14	–	–	6
1993		13	21	0	117	516	24.57	1	1	3
1993–94	Pak (Zim)	2	3	1	16*	42	21.00	–	–	1
	NZ	4	4	0	35	72	18.00	–	–	–
1994		6	10	0	98	244	24.40	–	2	–
1994–95	SL	3	3	0	37	78	26.00	–	–	2
	Pak (Aus)	2	4	1	45*	93	31.00	–	–	1
	SA	1	2	0	41	52	26.00	–	–	–
	Zim	4	5	0	27	51	10.20	–	–	2
1995		14	22	3	61	423	22.26	–	4	1
1995–96	Pak (SL)	2	3	0	36	64	21.33	–	–	2
	Aus	4	7	0	33	68	9.71	–	–	2
	NZ	1	2	0	19	21	10.50	–	–	–
1996	Pak in UK	7	9	1	68	211	26.37	–	1	4
1996–97	Pak (Zim)	2	2	1	257*	292	292.00	1	–	1
	Tasmania	1	2	0	29	29	14.50	–	–	–
1997		1	2	0	13	16	8.00	–	–	1
+1997–98	Pak (SA/WI)	7	6	0	59	86	14.33	–	1	3
TOTALS		204	277	31	257*	5466	22.21	5	19	69

SUMMARY OF ALL FIRST-CLASS MATCHES

Overs	Mdns	Runs	Wkts	Av	BB	5wI	10wM	S/R
80.5	18	222	13	17.07	7–50	1	–	37.30
122.4	30	302	12	25.16	5–56	2	1	61.33
9	3	21	1	21.00	1–21	–	–	54.00
176	38	495	12	41.25	2–17	–	–	87.99
143.3	56	291	12	24.25	4–55	–	–	71.75
37	5	112	6	18.66	6–91	1	–	37.00
184.2	35	487	14	34.78	5–96	1	–	79.00
394	82	1095	39	28.07	6–34	2	–	60.61
40.1	7	102	2	51.00	2–64	–	–	120.50
127	23	350	12	29.16	4–73	–	–	63.50
291.4	76	666	31	21.48	7–53	2	–	56.45
33.4	8	73	5	14.60	4–40	–	–	40.40
466.1	103	1117	63	17.73	7–42	7	2	44.39
204.4	50	551	18	30.61	5–101	1	–	68.22
135.4	37	318	17	18.70	6–62	3	1	47.88
204	44	640	16	40.00	3–76	–	–	76.50
184.5	36	460	31	14.83	5–28	1	–	35.77
429.3	99	1251	56	22.33	6–66	7	1	46.01
85	21	211	6	35.16	3–71	–	–	85.00
43.5	15	73	7	10.42	5–47	1	–	37.57
499.5	127	1330	82	16.21	6–32	7	2	36.57
45.5	7	143	10	14.30	6–53	1	1	27.50
93	24	199	11	18.09	5–45	1	–	50.72
146.1	22	491	14	35.07	4–75	–	–	62.64
409.2	93	1137	59	19.27	8–68	5	1	41.62
76.2	14	203	11	18.45	5–65	1	–	41.63
196.4	55	486	29	16.75	7–119	2	1	40.68
213.4	44	646	27	23.92	8–30	2	1	47.40
102.2	30	259	19	13.63	5–43	2	–	32.31
70.5	10	200	9	22.22	5–64	1	–	47.22
59	16	166	4	41.50	2–53	–	–	88.50
168.2	46	380	18	21.11	5–43	1	–	56.11
518.1	108	1598	81	19.72	7–52	7	3	38.38
43	12	110	9	12.22	5–55	1	–	28.66
160.4	39	375	20	18.75	4–43	–	–	48.20
35.5	7	84	5	16.80	5–53	1	–	43.00
271.5	67	787	32	24.59	5–58	1	–	50.96
71.4	21	180	11	16.36	6–48	1	1	39.09
10	4	34	2	17.00	2–34	–	–	30.00
36	10	86	3	28.66	3–74	–	–	72.00
178.1	52	464	28	16.57	4–42	–	–	38.17
6799.5	**1594**	**18195**	**857**	**21.23**	**8–30**	**63**	**15**	**47.60**

FIRST-CLASS CAREER SUMMARY

	M	I	NO	HS	Runs	Av	100	50	Ct
PACO	3	4	0	9	17	4.25	–	–	3
Lahore City Whites	2	1	0	5	5	5.00	–	–	–
PIA	2	3	0	59	77	25.66	–	1	1
BCCP Patron's XI	1	–	–	–	–	–	–	–	–
Pakistan Under-23	1	1	1	12*	12	–	–	–	–
Tests in Pakistan	32	38	6	257*	917	28.65	1	2	12
Pakistan in UK	35	38	6	68	755	23.59	–	2	16
Pakistan teams overseas	49	69	8	123	1032	16.91	1	3	22
Championship	76	119	9	122	2617	23.79	3	11	15
Lancashire other	2	3	0	18	20	6.66	–	–	–
World XI	1	1	1	14*	14	–	–	–	–
TOTALS	**204**	**277**	**31**	**257***	**5466**	**22.21**	**5**	**19**	**69**

FIVE WICKETS IN AN INNINGS

+ denotes 2nd innings; DEB denotes first-class debut; HT denotes Hat Trick included

1.	7–50	BCCP Patron's XI	New Zealand XI	Rawalpindi	1984–85	DEB
2.	5–56	PAKISTAN	NEW ZEALAND	AUCKLAND	1984–85	
3.	+5–72	PAKISTAN	NEW ZEALAND	AUCKLAND	1984–85	
4.	6–91	PAKISTAN	WEST INDIES	FAISALABAD	1986–87	
5.	5–96	PAKISTAN	INDIA	CALCUTTA	1986–87	
6.	+5–40	Pakistanis	Essex	Chelmsford	1987	
7.	6–34	Pakistanis	Middlesex	Lord's	1987	
8.	7–53	Lancashire	Northamptonshire	Northampton	1988	
9.	5–58	Lancashire	Surrey	Southport	1988	HT
10.	6–70	Lancashire	Nottinghamshire	Old Trafford	1989	
11.	5–52	Lancashire	Worcestershire	Worcester	1989	
12.	5–45	Lancashire	Glamorgan	Old Trafford	1989	
13.	5–44	Lancashire	Yorkshire	Old Trafford	1989	
14.	+5–51	Lancashire	Yorkshire	Old Trafford	1989	
15.	+5–52	Lancashire	Surrey	Old Trafford	1989	
16.	+7–42	World XI	MCC	Scarborough	1989	
17.	5–101	PAKISTAN	INDIA	SIALKOT	1989–90	
18.	6–62	PAKISTAN	AUSTRALIA	MELBOURNE	1989–90	
19.	+5–98	PAKISTAN	AUSTRALIA	MELBOURNE	1989–90	
20.	5–100	PAKISTAN	AUSTRALIA	ADELAIDE	1989–90	
21.	+5–28	PAKISTAN	WEST INDIES	LAHORE	1990–91	
22.	+5–48	Lancashire	Hampshire	Basingstoke	1991	
23.	+5–61	Lancashire	Leicestershire	Leicester	1991	
24.	+6–86	Lancashire	Kent	Old Trafford	1991	
25.	5–117	Lancashire	Nottinghamshire	Trent Bridge	1991	
26.	5–63	Lancashire	Middlesex	Uxbridge	1991	
27.	+6–66	Lancashire	Middlesex	Uxbridge	1991	
28.	5–91	Lancashire	Yorkshire	Old Trafford	1991	

FIRST-CLASS CAREER SUMMARY

Overs	Mdns	Runs	Wkts	Av	BB	5wI	10wM	S/R
85	14	284	6	47.33	3–70	–	–	85.00
44.1	7	108	5	21.60	3–30	–	–	53.00
60.5	14	169	12	14.08	6–53	1	1	30.41
39.5	10	104	9	11.55	7–50	1	–	26.55
9	3	21	1	21.00	1–21	–	–	54.00
1064.3	246	2788	134	20.80	6–48	7	1	47.66
1165.4	276	3212	153	20.99	6–32	10	2	45.71
1762.4	447	4368	201	21.73	7–119	14	3	52.61
2502	561	6971	322	21.64	8–30	29	7	46.62
33.3	5	102	4	25.50	2–35	–	–	50.25
32.4	11	68	10	6.80	7–42	1	1	19.60
6799.5	**1594**	**18195**	**857**	**21.23**	**8–30**	**63**	**15**	**47.60**

FIVE WICKETS IN AN INNINGS (continued)

29. +5–47	Pakistan XI	Victoria	Bendigo	1991–92
30. 5–43	Pakistanis	Northamptonshire	Northampton	1992
31. +5–74	Pakistanis	Northamptonshire	Northampton	1992
32. 5–128	PAKISTAN	ENGLAND	OLD TRAFFORD	1992
33. 5–59	Pakistanis	Derbyshire	Derby	1992
34. 6–67	PAKISTAN	ENGLAND	OVAL	1992
35. 5–44	Pakistanis	Gloucestershire	Bristol	1992
36. +6–32	Pakistanis	Gloucestershire	Bristol	1992
37. +6–53	PIA	PNSC	Multan	1992–93
38. +5–45	PAKISTAN	NEW ZEALAND	HAMILTON	1992–93
39. +6–49	Lancashire	Surrey	Oval	1993
40. +6–45	Lancashire	Derbyshire	Derby	1993
41. 8–68	Lancashire	Yorkshire	Old Trafford	1993
42. 5–69	Lancashire	Kent	Lytham St Anne's	1993
43. 5–63	Lancashire	Northamptonshire	Old Trafford	1993
44. +5–65	PAKISTAN	ZIMBABWE	RAWALPINDI	1993–94
45. +6–43	PAKISTAN	NEW ZEALAND	AUCKLAND	1993–94
46. +7–119	PAKISTAN	NEW ZEALAND	WELLINGTON	1993–94
47. 5–117	Lancashire	Somerset	Southport	1994
48. +8–30	Lancashire	Somerset	Southport	1994
49. 5–76	Pakistan XI	SL Board President's XI	Kurunegala	1994–95
50. +5–43	PAKISTAN	SRI LANKA	COLOMBO	1994–95
51. +5–64	PAKISTAN	AUSTRALIA	KARACHI	1994–95
52. +5–43	PAKISTAN	ZIMBABWE	BULAWAYO	1994–95
53. 5–40	Lancashire	Durham	Old Trafford	1995
54. 6–35	Lancashire	Middlesex	Lord's	1995
55. +7–73	Lancashire	Northamptonshire	Old Trafford	1995
56. 5–58	Lancashire	Gloucestershire	Cheltenham	1995

FIVE WICKETS IN AN INNINGS (continued)

57.	6–72	Lancashire	Leicestershire	Leicester	1995
58.	+6–93	Lancashire	Leicestershire	Leicester	1995
59.	7–52	Lancashire	Hampshire	Portsmouth	1995
60.	5–55	PAKISTAN	SRI LANKA	PESHAWAR	1995–96
61.	5–53	PAKISTAN	NEW ZEALAND	CHRISTCHURCH	1995–96
62.	5–58	Pakistanis	Northamptonshire	Northampton	1996
63.	6–48	PAKISTAN	ZIMBABWE	FAISALABAD	1996–97

TEN WICKETS IN A MATCH

1.	10–128	PAKISTAN	NEW ZEALAND	AUCKLAND	1984–85
2.	10–95	Lancashire	Yorkshire	Old Trafford	1989
3.	10–68	World XI	MCC	Scarborough	1989
4.	11–160	PAKISTAN	AUSTRALIA	MELBOURNE	1989–90
5.	11–129	Lancashire	Middlesex	Uxbridge	1991
6.	10–117	Pakistanis	Northamptonshire	Northampton	1992
7.	11–76	Pakistanis	Gloucestershire	Bristol	1992
8.	10–143	PIA	PNSC	Multan	1992–93
9.	12–125	Lancashire	Yorkshire	Old Trafford	1993
10.	11–179	PAKISTAN	NEW ZEALAND	WELLINGTON	1993–94
11.	13–147	Lancashire	Somerset	Southport	1994
12.	10–172	Lancashire	Northamptonshire	Old Trafford	1995
13.	12–165	Lancashire	Leicestershire	Leicester	1995
14.	10–156	Lancashire	Hampshire	Portsmouth	1995
15.	10–106	PAKISTAN	ZIMBABWE	FAISALABAD	1996–97

FIRST-CLASS HUNDREDS

+ denotes 2nd innings

1.	116*	Lancashire	Somerset	Old Trafford	1988
2.	+123	PAKISTAN	AUSTRALIA	ADELAIDE	1989–90
3.	122	Lancashire	Hampshire	Basingstoke	1991
4.	117	Lancashire	Derbyshire	Derby	1993
5.	257*	PAKISTAN	ZIMBABWE	SHEIKHUPURA	1996–97

PAIRS

| PAKISTAN | SRI LANKA | COLOMBO | 1985–86 |
| Lancashire | Gloucestershire | Cheltenham | 1995 |

HAT TRICKS

First-class (1)

1988	Lancashire	Surrey		Southport
	I A Greig	lbw	0	
	K T Medlycott	b	0	
	M A Feltham	b	0	

LIMITED-OVERS INTERNATIONALS (2)

14.10.1989	Pakistan	West Indies		Sharjah
	P J L Dujon	b	6	
	M D Marshall	b	0	
	C E L Ambrose	b	0	
4.5.1990	Pakistan	Australia		Sharjah
	M G Hughes	b	9	
	C G Rackemann	b	0	
	T M Alderman	b	0	

INTERNATIONAL LIMITED-OVERS MATCHES SUMMARY

Season	Opponent	M	I	NO	HS	Runs	Av	100	50	Ct
1984–85	NZ/I/A/WI/E	8	3	2	2	2	2.00	–	–	1
1985–86	WI/I/SL/NZ/									
	A/Bang	17	7	1	24	57	9.50	–	–	4
1986–87	WI/SL/I/A/E	19	12	3	48*	109	12.11	–	–	2
1987	Eng in UK	3	2	0	12	12	6.00	–	–	–
1987–88	World Cup	7	6	0	39	85	14.16	–	–	1
	E/WI	4	4	0	18	32	8.00	–	–	–
1988–89	WI/I/A/SL									
	Bang	15	14	3	17	93	8.45	–	–	7
1989–90	I/WI/E/A/SL									
	NZ	24	20	5	86	373	24.86	–	1	4
1990–91	SL	2	2	0	9	13	6.50	–	–	–
1991–92	I/WI/SL	13	12	2	19	102	10.20	–	–	4
	World Cup	10	8	2	33	62	10.33	–	–	1
1992	Eng in UK	4	4	1	34	73	24.33	–	–	1
1992–93	A/WI/NZ/Zim									
	SL/SA	27	24	3	39*	314	14.95	–	–	4
1993–94	I/UAE/NZ/WI									
	SL/Zim/NZ	16	12	4	33	140	17.50	–	–	3
1994–95	SL/A/SA/Zim									
	I/Bang	20	14	1	50	213	16.38	–	1	1
1995–96	NZ	4	4	1	36*	66	22.00	–	–	5
	World Cup	5	2	2	32*	60	–	–	–	1
1996	Eng in UK	3	3	0	21	32	10.66	–	–	1
1996–97	I/SA/Zim/SL									
	NZ/A/WI	31	28	3	66*	342	13.68	–	2	16
1997–98	SA/WI/SL/I/E	6	5	1	22	50	12.50	–	–	3
TOTALS		**238**	**186**	**34**	**86**	**2230**	**14.67**	**–**	**4**	**59**

COUNTRY BY COUNTRY

New Zealand		26	21	6	66*	359	23.93	–	2	8
India		33	26	5	50	272	12.95	–	1	10
Australia		30	26	3	86	453	19.69	–	1	3
England		25	20	3	34	187	11.00	–	–	5
West Indies		54	43	6	39*	364	9.83	–	–	16
Sri Lanka		38	29	5	39	338	14.08	–	–	9
Bangladesh		3	1	1	30*	30	–	–	–	–
Zimbabwe		14	10	3	38	81	11.57	–	–	6
South Africa		12	10	2	32*	146	18.25	–	–	1
United Arab Emirates		2	–	–	–	–	–	–	-	1
Holland		1	–	–	–	–	–	–	–	–
IN PAKISTAN		60	41	9	66*	519	16.21	–	2	14
OVERSEAS		178	145	25	86	1711	14.25	–	2	45
TOTALS		**238**	**186**	**34**	**86**	**2230**	**14.67**	**–**	**4**	**59**

INTERNATIONAL LIMITED-OVERS MATCHES SUMMARY

Overs	Mdns	Runs	Wkts	Av	BB	4wI	R.P.O.
58.3	3	230	9	25.55	5–21	1	3.93
118.1	16	429	25	17.16	4–19	2	3.63
174.4	23	613	24	25.54	3–26	–	3.50
30.4	3	112	3	37.33	2–18	–	3.65
63.2	2	295	7	42.14	3–45	–	4.65
29	2	118	4	29.50	3–25	–	4.06
129.5	4	542	24	22.58	4–25	1	4.17
201.2	17	723	34	21.26	5–38	1	3.59
18	2	59	3	19.66	2–40	–	3.27
106.4	7	458	16	28.62	3–27	–	4.29
89.4	3	338	18	18.77	4–32	1	3.76
41.4	3	180	4	45.00	2–41	–	4.32
244.4	19	898	44	20.40	5–16	6	3.67
135.1	10	482	31	15.54	5–15	3	3.56
192	14	687	27	25.44	3–20	–	3.57
36.2	1	117	9	13.00	3–18	–	3.22
33.2	3	135	3	45.00	2–25	–	4.05
29.4	2	140	6	23.33	3–45	–	4.71
259.4	23	966	42	23.00	4–25	3	3.72
50	2	242	8	30.25	4–33	1	4.84
2042.2	**159**	**7764**	**341**	**22.76**	**5–15**	**19**	**3.80**
201.5	19	707	46	15.36	5–19	3	3.50
279.3	25	1026	43	23.86	4–35	1	3.67
275.3	25	1084	44	24.63	5–21	3	3.93
223	15	903	29	31.13	3–25	–	4.04
459.1	28	1908	77	24.77	5–38	4	4.15
321.5	28	1190	51	23.33	4–24	4	3.69
25	5	54	6	9.00	4–19	1	2.16
116	8	372	21	17.71	5–15	1	3.20
113.3	3	446	19	23.47	5–116	2	3.92
17	2	44	5	8.80	3–19	–	2.58
10	1	30	–	–	–	–	3.00
457.1	29	1949	67	29.08	5–15	2	4.26
1585.1	130	5815	274	21.22	5–16	17	3.66
2042.2	**159**	**7764**	**341**	**22.76**	**5–15**	**19**	**3.80**

FIFTIES IN LIMITED-OVERS INTERNATIONALS

1.	86	Australia	Melbourne	23.2.1990
2.	50	India	Sharjah	7.4.1995
3.	52	New Zealand	Gujranwala	4.12.1996
4.	66*	New Zealand	Karachi	8.12.196

FOUR WICKETS IN AN INNINGS IN LIMITED-OVERS INTERNATIONALS

1.	5–21	Australia	Melbourne	20.2.1985
2.	4–28	Sri Lanka	Colombo	11.3.1986
3.	4–19	Bangladesh	Colombo	31.3.1986
4.	4–25	Australia	Perth	2.1.1989
5.	5–38	West Indies	Sharjah	14.10.1989
6.	4–32	New Zealand	Christchurch	18.3.1992
7.	4–46	West Indies	Perth	4.12.1992
8.	5–19	New Zealand	Wellington	26.12.1992
9.	4–24	Sri Lanka	Sharjah	2.2.1993
10.	4–24	Sri Lanka	Sharjah	4.2.1993
11.	5–16	South Africa	East London	15.2.1993
12.	4–18	West Indies	St Vincent	30.3.1993
13.	4–40	West Indies	Sharjah	1.11.1993
14.	5–15	Zimbabwe	Karachi	24.12.1993
15.	4–23	New Zealand	Auckland	6.3.1994
16.	4–35	India	Toronto	19.9.1996
17.	4–42	Sri Lanka	Sharjah	8.11.1996
18.	4–25	Australia	Melbourne	16.1.1997
19.	4–33	South Africa	Lahore	2.11.1997

DOMESTIC LIMITED-OVERS SUMMARY

	M	I	NO	HS	Runs	Av	50	Ct
Sundays 1988–1997	94	75	19	51*	1250	22.32	2	20
Benson & Hedges 1988–1997	31	24	5	64	538	28.31	3	2
NatWest	17	14	3	50	192	17.45	1	5
TOTALS	142	113	27	64	1980	23.02	6	27

Note: No matches in 1992 or 1996 because of Pakistan tours of UK

Highest Score Sunday	51*	Yorkshire	Old Trafford	22.8.1993
Highest Score B&H	64	Worcestershire	Worcester	13.6.1995
Highest Score NatWest	50	Surrey	Oval	6.7.1994

HAT TRICKS IN LIMITED-OVERS INTERNATIONALS

1.	West Indies	Sharjah	14.10.1989	Dujon, Marshall, Ambrose
2.	Australia	Sharjah	4.5.1990	Hughes, Rackemann, Alderman

FOUR WICKETS IN AN INNINGS IN LIMITED-OVERS MATCHES

1.	4–27	Lincolnshire	Old Trafford	22.6.1988	NatWest
2.	5–27	Scotland	Perth	2.5.1989	B&H
3.	4–54	Essex	Chelmsford	31.5.1989	B&H
4.	4–30	Surrey	Old Trafford	27.8.1989	Sunday
5.	4–39	Gloucestershire	Old Trafford	10.6.1990	Sunday
6.	4–34	Derbyshire	Derby	11.7.1990	NatWest
7.	4–19	Yorkshire	Scarborough	5.8.1990	Sunday
8.	4–18	Sussex	Old Trafford	7.5.1991	B&H
9.	4–32	Surrey	Oval	6.6.1993	Sunday
10.	5–10	Leicestershire	Leicester	8.6.1993	B&H
11.	4–20	Sussex	Old Trafford	20.6.1993	Sunday
12.	5–41	Northamptonshire	Northampton	5.6.1994	Sunday
13.	4–29	Northamptonshire	Old Trafford	9.7.1995	Sunday
14.	4–16	Sussex	Old Trafford	6.8.1995	Sunday

FIFTIES IN DOMESTIC LIMITED-OVERS MATCHES

1.	52	Northamptonshire	Northampton	9.5.1989	B&H
2.	50	Glamorgan	Colwyn Bay	27.5.1990	Sunday
3.	51*	Yorkshire	Old Trafford	22.8.1993	Sunday
4.	50	Surrey	Oval	6.7.1994	NatWest
5.	64	Worcestershire	Worcester	13.6.1995	B&H
6.	52*	Warwickshire	Edgbaston	2.5.1997	B&H

DOMESTIC LIMITED-OVERS SUMMARY

Overs	Mdns	Runs	Wkts	Av	BB	4wI	R.P.O.	MM
676.4	26	2914	151	19.29	5–41	8	4.30	–
306.5	26	1208	59	20.47	5–10	3	3.93	3
181.4	21	681	23	29.60	4–27	2	3.74	–
1165.1	**73**	**4803**	**233**	**20.61**	**5–10**	**13**	**4.12**	**3**

Best Bowling Sunday	5–41	Northamptonshire	Northampton	5.6.1994
Best Bowling B&H	5–10	Leicestershire	Leicester	8.6.1993
Best Bowling NatWest	4–27	Lincolnshire	Old Trafford	22.6.1988

Index